Bush Versus Chávez

Bush Versus Chávez

Washington's War on Venezuela

Eva Golinger

MONTHLY REVIEW PRESS
NEW YORK

Library of Congress Cataloging-in-Publication Data

Golinger, Eva.
  Bush Verses Chávez : Washington's war on Venezuela / Eva Golinger.
    p. cm.
      ISBN 978-1-58367-166-5 (hardback) — ISBN 978-1-58367-165-8 (pbk.)

1. United States—Foreign relations—Venezuela. 2. Venezuela—Foreign rela-
tions—United States. 3. Chávez Frías, Hugo. 4. Bush, George W. (George
Walker), 1946 – 5. Venezuela—Politics and government—1999 – 6. Venezuela—
History—Attempted coup, 2002. I. Title.

E183.8.V4G65 2007
327.73087—dc22
                    2007034736

Design by Terry J. Allen

Monthly Review Press
146 West 29th Street – Suite 6W
New York, NY 10001

http://www.monthlyreview.org

10 9 8 7 6 5 4 3 2 1

Contents

*Dedicated to the memory of the more than
160 Venezuelan campesinos who have lost their lives
in the struggle to defend their land,
their families, and their future.*

Acknowledgments

This book could never have been written without the tremendous love and endless showings of respect and appreciation I've received from the brave and beautiful people of Venezuela. The warmth, generosity, and kindness from countless souls in this nation have served to shield and protect me from the threats, dangers, and risks involved in investigating U.S. intervention and CIA activities in Venezuela. I am eternally thankful for that. *Bush Verses Chávez: Washington's War on Venezuela* is the result of more than two years of investigations that still continue, and the contributions of many dear friends and compañeros y compañeras.

First and foremost thanks to Jeremy Bigwood, for continuing arduous FOIA work from within the depths of the empire; to my mom, dad, and brother for unconditional love and support and for trekking down to Venezuela to visit me to make sure that I am safe and happy; to my dearest little furry Lola, the best company a girl could have; to the Generals Baduel, Carvajal, Lameda, Lopez Hidalgo, Morgado, Ortega, and Rangel, for trusting me and contributing to uncovering the truth—count me as a loyal soldier in your battalions; to Mayor Balza and Isa, for moral support and confidence; to Abel, Iroel, Polanco, Carlitos, Felix, Richard, and the translation team, as well as the Comandante and unnamed compañeros, for their heartfelt generosity, solidarity, and humanity; to Angel and Rigoberto for hard work, great analysis, and commitment; to all the bodyguards who have been with me, occasionally, throughout the past two years: Benitez, Mendoza, Maestro Rodriguez, Arístides, and the rest, I am indebted to you all for risking your lives to protect me; to Mario and La Hojilla for always providing space for me to speak truths and denounce the latest strategies of the empire; to RNV, Diario Reporte, and Mandinga, for publishing my articles and letting my voice be heard; to all the different institutions, ministries, units of the armed forces, organizations, and groups that have invited me to speak and treated me with respect and affection; and to my beloved friends and allies who have helped me laugh when I wanted to cry and have given me the strength to keep this fight alive: Celia, Lely, Gretchen, Roselena, Catherine, Skipper, Temir, Piki, Ernesto, Juan Carlos, Daniel, Michel Collon, Livia, Angel P., Maria Mercedes, Leon, and all the friendly faces that smile and wave to me as I pass by. Special thanks to President Hugo Chávez, Vice President José Vicente Rangél, Attorney General Isaias Rodriguéz, Centro Internacional Miranda, Casa Militar, la Universidad Bolivariana de Venezuela, DIM, DISIP, Nicolás Maduro, Mari Pili Hernández, Yuri Pimentel, Andrés, Samuel Moncada, Monte Avila Editores, Zambon, MCI, Menry Fernandéz, Juan Barreto, Cooperativa Humana, Tiuna el Fuerte, and the rest of the crew who struggle every day to make this revolution a reality.

You can all count on me, always.

Introduction

After writing *The Chávez Code: Cracking U.S. Intervention in Venezuela,* I was flooded with information from sources all around the world about the evildoings of the Bush administration in Venezuela and elsewhere. *The Chávez Code* was almost entirely based on documents my colleague, journalist and photographer Jeremy Bigwood, and I obtained through use of the U.S. Freedom of Information Act (FOIA) in the United States directly from the U.S. government. *Bush Verses Chávez: Washington's War on Venezuela* is based on a variety of additional information, testimonies, and data I have been given from private sources. Jeremy and I continue our FOIA requests, despite increasing censorship from the Bush administration.

Since the publication of *The Chávez Code,* we have received more than a thousand new documents evidencing U.S. intervention in Venezuela, and much of that information is incorporated in this new text.

Methodology

The FOIA is a body of law passed after the end of the Nixon administration that enables journalists and others to access and declassify secret U.S. government documents. Information requested through the FOIA is first analyzed by the government agency possessing the relevant documentation, which may release or withhold part or all of it.

There are many different entities within the U.S. government, and in order to find out how deeply involved the United States has been in

Venezuela, it was necessary to file hundreds of requests with agencies ranging from the Department of State to the Department of Defense, Department of the Army, U.S. SOUTHCOM, Department of Agriculture, National Endowment for Democracy, U.S. Agency for International Development, and others. The investigation, which was initiated in 2003, continues to the present time and most likely will extend for decades to come. Generally, the U.S. government takes a long time to respond to FOIA requests and typically engages in delay tactics and censoring intended to prevent information from reaching the public at large. Often, documents or information withheld or unlawfully delayed can be appealed, but the appeals process can continue for an indeterminate period, therefore hampering critical information from reaching public scrutiny.

FOIA investigations generally occur years or decades after the U.S. intervention has occurred, such as the case of Chile, often when it is too late to act in a preventive or precautionary manner. This investigation, however, is occurring in "real time" and therefore has the privileged opportunity of effecting change on U.S. policy in Venezuela. To date, the results of the investigation have already influenced U.S.-Venezuela relations and have also opened the eyes of millions of Venezuelans who were unaware of the extent of U.S. meddling in their nation. The details of what the investigation has uncovered were published in full in *The Chávez Code: Cracking U.S. Intervention in Venezuela,* and are updated in the pages that follow.

Background on U.S. Intervention in Venzuela 2001–04

There was a bloody coup d'état on April 11, 2002, in Venezuela similar to the overthrow of the Allende government in Chile nearly thirty years earlier. An unlikely bond between labor unions, business associations, and the elite military command was formed with a common goal: to remove President Hugo Chávez Frías from his elected office. In a stark contrast to Chilean history, the coup in Venezuela failed and two days later President Chávez was reinstated. Yet the details surrounding the events remain murky and confusing, and tall tales of human rights abuses, authoritarian-type actions, and peaceful protests by a falsified majority overshadow the facts.

What really happened during those three days that changed Venezuelan history forever? A coup led by a joint force of corrupt labor leaders, corporate interests, media moguls, and high military command really did try to overthrow President Chávez. The private media in Venezuela, which is owned by a corporate elite, played a key role in manipulating information and news about the developing events, misleading Venezuelans and international followers into believing that the Chávez government had openly fired on opposition demonstrators, therefore justifying the coup. Pedro Carmona, then president of Fedecámaras, Venezuela's chamber of commerce, assumed the position of "interim president" of the nation and quickly dissolved all of Venezuela's core democratic institutions. A select group of 395 representatives from the Venezuelan elite stood by at the Presidential Palace and endorsed Carmona's decree, legitimizing his "dictatorship" on April 12, 2002.[1]

In the United States, the Bush administration expressed its support for the Carmona government and refused to recognize that a military-corporate coup had occurred. Instead, the United States blamed the violence and instability on the Chávez government and claimed President Chávez had resigned from his elected office.[2] Behind the scenes, high level U.S. State Department officials in Caracas, such as Otto Reich, Elliot Abrams, and Ambassador Charles Shapiro, met several times with Pedro Carmona and other coup leaders, before, during, and after the events of April 11.[3] The U.S. stood practically alone in its recognition of Carmona as a legitimate head of state. The Organization of American States, CARICOM, and nations of the European Union, with the exception of Spain, all issued statements or comments condemning the coup and refusing to acknowledge Carmona as President of Venezuela.

On April 13, 2002, when President Chávez was returned to power by a popular uprising and support from within the military barracks, the U.S. was forced to publicly retract the unconditional support it had given to the coup leaders. Yet the headstrong Bush administration continued to blame Chávez for the preceding events and merely claimed that his return as president was a "second opportunity" to try to correct his policies and make good with the U.S., i.e., succumb to U.S. power.[4]

President Hugo Chávez was elected by approximately 60 percent of the vote in 1998, defeating Venezuela's traditional two parties, Acción

Democrática (AD) and COPEI (Social Christian Party of Venezuela), by a landslide. He appealed to a cross-section of Venezuelan society in that first election, primarily because he offered an alternative to the corrupt AD and COPEI parties that had ruled the nation for forty years and had run the economy into the ground by the late 1990s. But Chávez's immediate implementation of his campaign promises, including a restructuring of the state-owned oil company PDVSA, and a redrafting of Venezuela's young constitution, proved too radical and abrupt for many Venezuelans accustomed to life under AD and COPEI, where promises were abandoned and structural change was spoken of but never implemented.

Despite shock from some sectors at the swiftness of the Chávez administration's actions, more than 70 percent of the electorate participated in drafting and ratifying a new constitution in 1999 that would authorize sweeping changes in Venezuelan society. As a result of new constitutional terms, presidential elections were held again in 1999 and Chávez won with a similar 60 percent margin. With the authority of the 1999 constitution behind him, Chávez was able to initiate a series of structural changes within PDVSA that would enable a more equal distribution of the company's profits and, in turn, provide income for social programs intended to decrease poverty and ensure social services for Venezuela's vast low and no income population.

During the period of 1998–2000, Chávez encountered an indifferent U.S. policy toward Venezuela. It wasn't until George W. Bush arrived at the White House in 2000 that relations between Venezuela and the United States took a turn for the worse. Chávez administration policies did not sit well with the Bush administration. The idea that a government in charge of one of the most important oil industries in the world liaised closely and openly with Fidel Castro was a difficult pill to swallow for a Republican administration that had again tightened the noose around the Cuban economy with the forty-year-old goal of ousting Castro. Furthermore, Chávez's revitalization of the Organization of Petroleum Exporting Countries (OPEC), an entity the U.S. would have preferred muted, and his visits to fellow oil-producing countries, such as Libya and Iraq, rubbed the Bush administration the wrong way. Not to mention the Venezuelan government's focus on policies to reduce poverty and promote a participatory democracy, ideas repulsed by diehard market economists. Factor in a disgruntled and wealthy Venezuelan business elite with friends in high places in the U.S. government and corporate world, and a clear dislike for the Chávez government was clinched.

The overt statements and declarations made by U.S. government officials indicating a tendency to break relations with the Chávez administration began in early 2001. After President Chávez expressed his disagreement and outrage to the bombings in Afghanistan post-9/11, relations between the Bush and Chávez administrations quickly deteriorated. Chávez was not playing by the "you are either with us or against us" rules and his country was too important to leave in the hands of such a disobedient actor.

The Intervention

U.S. intervention in Venezuela from 2001 to 2004 was implemented in three stages, each adapting to the circumstances presented by the failure of the previous attempt to garner any success. Beginning in 2005, a new strategy was approached, one more hostile, public, and aggressive that has increased the notion of U.S. meddling in Venezuela from mere "intervention" to "war." The U.S. strategy in Venezuela has followed a textbook outline of intervention in Latin America. The tactics used in Venezuela appear to have metamorphosed from those previously applied in Chile (1970s), Nicaragua (1980s), Haiti (1990s and 2004), and Cuba (1960–present). These resulted in the ouster of democratically elected presidents, either through coups d'état (Chile and Haiti) or heavily influenced electoral processes (Nicaragua), or they economically sabotaged the nation (Cuba) and produced an ongoing low-intensity conflict filled with subversion and aggression.

A Brief Note on the Chile Parallel

The past few years in Venezuela have shown common histories with Chile during the late 1960s and early 1970s. The coup and strikes that plagued Chile have also beleaguered Venezuela, yet the latter was able to resist and overcome the attempts of the right-wing opposition movement, which was financed and politically backed by the U.S. government. Chile, unfortunately, was forced to succumb to a violent takeover that resulted in the assassination of a democratically elected and popularly supported president, Salvador Allende, and instituted one of the most brutal dictatorships in Latin American history. The bloodied hands of the U.S. government left their stamp all over the 1973 coup in Chile, and later declassified documents attained by the National Security Archive revealed the intricate plots that Henry Kissinger and his cohorts had enacted to crush the growth of socialism in the region.

In Chile, the U.S. employed tactics that have subsequently proven successful time and time again. Before the coup, the U.S. had succeeded in funneling hundreds of thousands of dollars to labor unions, business associations, and social organizations willing to band together to oppose Allende. The U.S. attempted to prevent Allende's election in 1970 by strengthening and supporting opposition parties and candidates, but the overwhelming popularity of the socialist leader left the U.S. government with little choice but to go the violent route. Still, after Allende's election, the U.S. instigated acts of economic sabotage through massive strikes led by its financed counterparts and it attempted to isolate the Allende government from the international community. The U.S. also applied a strategy, later known as "Chileanization," which involved organizing internal right-wing forces to destabilize the elected government. This concept ensured that as opposition forces incited violent confrontations with the government, outrage would form in the international community over "Allende crackdowns," the nation would be portrayed in a state of civil disorder and instability, and the government would be labeled a "human rights violator" or international pariah. It wasn't until all these efforts had failed three years later that the coup plan proceeded forward.

The tactics used in Chile were preserved for future use by the U.S. government. The embarrassment of some members of Congress over the U.S. role in the overthrow of a democratically elected president and its unconditional support for a brutal dictator who went on to commit human rights atrocities for more than a decade merely affected the tone of future interventions, not the substance. In Venezuela, the U.S. applied many of the same tactics it had used in Chile—the formation of a movement bringing together labor unions, business associations, political parties and social organizations, the economic sabotage and the strikes. And of course, the bloody coup. But the failure of this strategy to take root in Venezuela led the U.S. government to alter its tactics, to merge together strategies it had successfully applied in other Latin American nations and to modernize its methodology.

It seems almost surprising that in the year 2002 the U.S. government would conceive of instigating a coup d'état to remove a democratically elected leader. Yet a quick glance at the U.S. administration at the time of the coup in Venezuela and particularly those individuals overseeing Latin American policy provides a plausible answer. Many of the same figures present during the coup in Chile or later during the armed conflict and intervention in Nicaragua and other Central American and Caribbean nations are today setting policy in the Bush administration. Individuals such as Otto Reich, Roger Noriega, Charles Shapiro, William Brownfield, Luigi Enaudi, John Negroponte, Elliot Abrams, and others all made their bones on Latin America in the 1970s and 1980s. Clearly, there are no lessons learned for these fellows. Even after the failed coup in Venezuela in 2002, the U.S. government instigated the overthrow of Jean Bertrand Aristide, the elected president of Haiti, in early 2004, this time successfully.

U.S. intervention strategy in Venezuela has adapted to its circumstances. Quickly picking itself up after the failure of the Chilean intervention model in Venezuela, the U.S. moved on to more modern and sophisticated tactics.

The National Endowment for Democracy

In the late 1970s, the American Political Foundation (APF), a coalition of labor, business, political and academic leaders, formed with the objective of seeking new methods of achieving U.S. foreign policy goals abroad, despite the congressional restrictions in place. The APF, funded by Congress and composed of ultra-conservative think tanks, such as the Center for Strategic and International Studies and the American Enterprise Institute, together with representatives from the National Security Council (NSC) and the USIA, the propaganda office of the U.S. government, proposed the creation of an institution funded by Congress to provide financial and political support to groups and organizations working for U.S. interests abroad. The institution would focus on "promoting democracy" through financial support intended to foster the "infrastructure of democracy" that would enable a free press, unions, political parties, universities and social organizations to function in the interests of U.S. foreign policy.

In 1983, as a result of APF recommendations, the National Endowment for Democracy (NED) was established by congressional legislation, the National Endowment for Democracy Act (P.L. 98-164), and Congress authorized funding to ensure its success. At the time of NED's creation, the APF had also recommended the formation of "core grantees" to act as funnels for congressional funds to reach political parties and partisan groups in other nations. The core grantees, which included the Center for International Private Enterprise (CIPE), the National Democratic Institute (NDI), the International Republican Institute (IRI), and the Free Trade Union Institute, which was connected to the AFL-CIO and later known as the American Center for International Labor Solidarity (ACILS), were all connected through an interlocking board of directors that shared influence within NED and the U.S. Congress.[5]

NED was created to serve as the perfect conduit for U.S. government funds to provide international political aid that would support its interests abroad and influence foreign and domestic policy in nations of strategic importance. Established during the Cold War, NED reflected a neoconservative agenda that prioritized its global struggle against communism over democratic notions of sovereignty and self-determination. Hence, NED's premiere in Nicaragua provided a major dose of U.S. intervention on a political and electoral level and its technique was perfected over the course of nearly a decade.

In Nicaragua, the CIA had originally been the principal conduit for financing the anti-Sandinista movement (the Contras), but after their failure to unseat the Sandinistas during the 1984 elections, NED was employed to ensure success on the 1989–90 ballot. During the 1984 elections, the U.S. was so sure of their defeat that they advocated for widespread voter abstention on the opposition side in order to discredit the elections, a move which, despite U.S. power and influence, still failed.

Therefore, the second time around the U.S. decided
role in the electoral process. Through the formation
movement composed of social organizations, political p
affiliates, the U.S. government was able to foment and con
of the Nicaraguan elections. The U.S. pushed for the unific
ious political parties and social organizations that opposed the
Sandinistas, many of which were far right and shared conservative agendas
with the Reagan administration. The U.S. made financing through NED to
these organizations contingent upon their formation of a unified group, the
Coordinadora Democrática Nicaragüense (CDN), capable of winning the
1989–90 elections. CDN was composed of four conservative political parties, two trade union groupings affiliated with the AFL-CIO, and a private
business organization, COSEP, that had close links to influential U.S. corporations and figures in the business community. Nearing the elections,
NED blackmailed the fourteen opposition parties in Nicaragua into forming one party, UNO, that would endorse the U.S.-chosen candidate,
Violeta Chamorro, for the presidency.

The U.S. could not afford another loss in Nicaragua against the
Sandinistas and, this time around, the effort was a "no holds barred" full-
fledged electoral intervention to ensure the U.S.-selected candidate would
assume the presidency. The CIA had been financing Nicaragua's main
newspaper, *La Prensa,* during the Sandinista-Contra war, and passed on
the baton to NED and its international affiliates during the late 1980s.
Control of media was a major tool in the propaganda war intended to not
only win over supporters internally in Nicaragua, but also to filter news and
information to the international press with a guaranteed anti-Sandinista and
pro-U.S. spin. The Venezuelan government, then headed by Carlos Andrés
Pérez (in his second term), played a major role in the funneling of funds and
support from the U.S. government to the CDN, UNO, and *La Prensa.*

Carlos Andrés Pérez had developed close ties to the Chamorro family
while in exile in Costa Rica during the Pérez Jiménez dictatorship in
Venezuela. He additionally had ties to other influential Nicaraguans, devel-
oped during his first presidential term from 1976 to 1980. Carlos Andrés
Pérez was eager to offer Venezuela's support for the U.S. efforts to oust the
Sandinista government through the strengthening of an anti-Sandinista civil

opposition. Beginning in 1989, the CIA rerouted a minimum of $200,000 monthly through Venezuelan private foundations destined to fund *La Prensa* and campaign materials for UNO. Carlos Andrés Pérez maintained close contact with President Bush during the electoral process in Nicaragua and even appointed his secretary of the presidency, Beatríz Rángel, as his personal representative in his contacts with Bush. According to one source, Rángel was observed carrying a suitcase "stuffed with secret funds from Washington and Miami to Caracas" destined for the Nicaraguan opposition's campaign.[6]

Venezuela's largest union, the Confederación de Trabajadores Venezolanos (CTV), worked in connection with NED and the AFL-CIO to establish ties with workers and unions in Nicaragua, with the goal of incorporating them into the opposition movement.[7] Carlos Andrés Pérez also recommended the use of the U.S. firm Penn and Schoen Associates to conduct a polling program in Nicaragua as part of the electoral intervention agenda. Penn and Schoen had done polling for Carlos Andrés Pérez's presidential campaign together with the Venezuelan firm DOXA and had also been used successfully as part of U.S. electoral intervention in Panamá. Penn and Schoen later became the polling firm of choice for these types of interventions and have subsequently been used in the former Yugoslavia during the elections that ousted Milosovic from power and, more recently, in Venezuela, during the recall referendum against President Chávez on August 15, 2004. In Venezuela, Penn and Schoen came under international scrutiny for allegedly producing fraudulent exit poll results conducted with Venezuelan NED-grantee Súmate that were intended to discredit the official results of the referendum.

The Venezuela connection with NED and CIA intervention in Nicaragua in the late 1980s proves the strong bond that was formed between those entities and politicians involved in the actions of that period. Such relationships have been integral in recent interventions pursued by the U.S. government in Venezuela during the Chávez era. Carlos Andrés Pérez has played an interesting role in three U.S. interventions in Venezuela and continues to act as a liaison between influential individuals in the United States from the Reagan-Bush era and opposition leaders in Venezuela, as a source of funds to those who led the coup against Chávez, and as an international propagandist spreading harsh critiques of the Chávez administration.

The major U.S. investment and intervention in Nicaragua was successful. In 1990, Violeta Chamorro was declared the winner of the elections and the Sandinistas were officially removed from power. As a result of the layers and networks the United States had built to cover its influential role in the electoral process, the elections were widely viewed as "transparent and democratic" and were accepted internationally. Satisfied with the outcome of its efforts, the United States proceeded to expand and implement its new "democratic intervention" model in other nations.

U.S. Agency for International Development

Another entity that existed prior to the Nicaragua intervention and that was also utilized to enable financing of U.S. interests abroad is the United States Agency for International Development (USAID), established by the U.S. Congress in 1961. USAID was originally intended to aid humanitarian development around the world but, similar to NED, had large portions of its funds diverted to support foreign political movements aligned with U.S. interests. Though USAID was created to separate military aid from humanitarian and development aid, it became an additional fund for the CIA to dip into for covert interventions. USAID's annual budget is much larger than NED's, but the funds still originate from the U.S. Congress. USAID is overseen and directed by the Department of State, which exercises complete authority over its actions.

One of the first misuses of USAID funds was during the early 1960s in Brazil. The CIA was heavily involved in attempts to stop João Goulart from succeeding in the Brazilian presidency because he was viewed as "leftist-leaning" and supported "social and economic reforms" that in the eyes of the CIA had communism written all over them. The CIA and USAID spent approximately $20 million to support hundreds of anti-Goulart candidates for gubernatorial elections in 1962. USAID was also used to invest heavily in the Brazilian labor movement. The funds were filtered through the international branch of the AFL-CIO, then the American Institute for Free Labor

Development (AIFLD), now known as the American Center for International Labor Solidarity (ACILS), and were controlled on the ground by the CIA. In 1964, President Goulart was overthrown by a CIA-backed coup that resulted in a brutal U.S.-sponsored dictatorship lasting twenty years.[8]

In the 1980s, as part of the move toward "democratic intervention" models, the Department of State established the USAID Office of Democratic Initiatives, with the goal of supporting and "strengthening democratic institutions." From 1984 to 1987, USAID utilized the office to filter more than $25 million into electoral processes in Latin America. Although NED later assumed similar operations, USAID has continued to use the office, now known as the Office of Transition Initiatives (OTI), to intervene in nations involved in crises that "threaten democracy." At the same time, USAID and NED overlap in funding initiatives for the International Republican Institute and the National Democratic Institute, both core NED grantees. In most instances, the USAID and NED funds provide financial assistance for electoral processes.

Venezuela

Venezuela's turmoil has been created in large part by the work of NED and USAID and their overseers. Similar to its role in Chile, Nicaragua, Haiti, Panamá, and the Philippines, among other nations, the United States has applied its successful model of "democratic intervention," which has involved the filtering of funds into opposition groups and political parties and the essential political training that enables its counterparts to success-fully obtain their objective. However, despite adapting to new realities in Venezuela and an unexpectedly strong populace that supports its govern-ment, the U.S. line of attack has been staved off each time it has been launched. Therefore, the three stages of intervention during 2001–04—the coup, the strike and the referendum—were unsuccessful, but the tactical and methodological undermining of the Chávez administration has evolved and adapted each time to its new setting.

Within each separate stage, a similar methodology has been utilized that involves several time-tested strategies intended to justify the final result:

removing Chávez from power. These tactics, which have been utilized previously in Chile and Nicaragua, for example, include:

- Isolating Chávez from the international community

- Exploiting the tensions between government, political parties, and civil society

- Exploiting the problems faced by the nation to place blame on the Chávez government

- Nurturing the opposition to Chávez to build a solid anti-Chávez movement

- Financing and politically encouraging and enabling the opposition to Chávez

- Conducting a media campaign to discredit Chávez's image and empower the opposition[9]

- Imposing an "environment of war" on the greater population through mass media overplaying conflict scenarios[10]

- Charging the Chávez government with human rights abuses and denouncing such alleged abuses in the international community without providing real evidence to support claims[11]

- Associating the Chávez government with supporting terrorist groups and networks[12]

- Discrediting and destroying the image of President Chávez

- Threatening the Chávez administration with potential "hostile" treatment from the U.S. government

All of the above tactics have been used by the U.S. government in prior interventions in Latin America and worldwide. In Chile, as explained previously, an opposition movement that brought together unlikely allies among labor and business and military was nurtured and financed for years before Allende's overthrow. Nicaragua saw a decade-long U.S.-imposed conflict that ultimately was able to achieve its goal via elections.

Three Stages of Intervention from 2001 to 2004

I
THE COUP

Months before the 2002 coup, the U.S. government had put into action a skillfully devised plan to aid the anti-Chávez movement in its objectives. An opposition to Chávez had been loosely formed between unlikely allies that included Venezuela's largest labor union, the Confederación de Trabajadores Venezolanos (CTV), the Chamber of Commerce (FEDECA-MARAS), and leaders from the traditional political parties, Acción Democrática, COPEI, Movimiento al Socialismo, and others. Despite their differences, these groups shared a common disagreement with the Chávez administration's policies based on their own loss of political and economic power resulting from the change of government. This opposition, including the CTV, was primarily composed of individuals and organizations stemming from Venezuela's elite, or as it is commonly referred to in Venezuela, the "oligarchy."

History shows that this wasn't the first time for an alliance between the CTV, Fedecámaras, and the traditional political parties. In the late 1980s, during Carlos Andrés Pérez's generous collaboration with the U.S. government, these same entities came together to form the National Democratic Foundation, which was used to funnel NED monies from the U.S. to Nicaragua. So once again, labor, business and political parties were unified to promote U.S. interests in Latin America.

NED had been present in Venezuela, though minimally, since the late 1980s when they began financing the CTV. But from 2000 to 2001, NED's budget in Venezuela quadrupled and funding began flowing into large and small organizations that all shared a common characteristic: aversion to President Chávez. NED gave out approximately $850,000 to "promote democracy" in Venezuela. Recipients included several Venezuelan organizations that were awarded direct grants from NED with no intermediaries and numerous other organizations that were given funding through the four NED core grantees—IRI, NDI, CIPE, and ACILS. Some of the groups directly funded by NED included the Asamblea de Educación (Education Assembly), Fundación Momento de la Gente (People's Moment

Foundation), which received a whopping $250,500, Asociación Civil Comprensión de Venezuela (Venezuelan Civil Association for Understanding), and the Asociación Civil Consorcio Justicia (Justice Consortium). During that same period, the International Republican Institute received $339,998 for its work with political parties such as Primero Justicia, AD, COPEI, and Proyecto Venezuela—all opposition parties—as did the National Democratic Institute, which received a total of $250,500 for its work with the same political parties as the IRI, in addition to its collaborations with the Fundación Momento de la Gente. The ACILS was awarded more than $150,000 for its work with the CTV in the months before the coup.

In the years 2000, 1999, and prior, the primary recipients of NED funds in Venezuela were the ACILS for its work with the CTV, CIPE for its work with counterpart Centro de Divulgación del Conocimiento Económico (CEDICE, Center for the Dissemination of Economic Information), and the IRI for its ongoing training and shaping of political parties in the nation. Direct NED grantees in Venezuela during those years included groups such as Centro al Servicio de la Acción Popular (CESAP, Center for the Service of Public Action), Programa para el Desarrollo Legislativo (PRODEL, Program for Legislative Development), Fundación Momento de la Gente, and Sinergia, an organization dedicated to strengthening other social organizations aligned with the opposition. All of these entities have leanings toward the opposition, some more than others. Even so, the NED role in Venezuela was relatively minor prior to 2001, when the Bush administration increased spending on organizations capable of forming a solid opposition movement to Chávez.

On December 10, 2001, the first "general strike" was called by the loose coalition of the CTV, Fedecámaras, private media, NED-funded social organizations, and opposition political parties to oppose the Chávez government's proposal of 49 new laws that would implement many of the new rights represented in the 1999 constitution. Prior to the strike, high-level officials of the U.S. government, including Colin Powell, George Tenet, and Roger Noriega, had made statements indicating a possible break in relations with the Chávez administration, basing such attitudes on Chávez's overt opposition to the bombing of Afghanistan in October 2001. In November

2001, the U.S. government called back its ambassador to Venezuela, Donna Hrinak, to Washington, generally an indicator of a change in relations. In December 2001, Charles Shapiro was sent to Caracas as the new U.S. ambassador to Venezuela. Shapiro's history with the State Department clearly provided evidence as to the tone the United States now chose to set with Venezuela. Shapiro had worked in the U.S. embassy in Chile during the coup against Allende, had later served as ambassador to El Salvador during the tumultuous '80s, and from 1999 to 2001 was director of the Bureau of Cuban Affairs office.

The December 10 strike paralyzed the nation for one day and set the stage for the months to come. The opposition organized multiple protests and acts of civil disobedience, and a faction of senior military officers began to "defect" and publicly declare a state of rebellion. The private media upped its tone of aggression toward the government and gave 100 percent coverage to the opposition, rarely presenting balanced news accounts. In March 2002, the International Republic Institute was given a $300,000 grant from NED to "strengthen political parties" in Venezuela. IRI had hand-selected Primero Justicia as its prime counterpart in Venezuela, and since 1999 had been crafting this young political party into becoming one of the most vocally opposed to the Chávez government. Primero Justicia had originally formed as a nonprofit social organization and was converted into a right-wing political party about the same time that IRI began receiving big NED grants to engage in party strengthening in Venezuela. Taking advantage of the lack of leadership and popularity of the traditional parties in Venezuela, Primero Justicia had successfully landed itself key political positions, including National Assembly seats and several municipal mayor offices in the wealthier sectors of Caracas.

At the same time that NED was pumping funds to key members of the opposition coalition, the U.S. embassy in Caracas was sending signs up to Washington that a change in government was soon likely and the man to fill the president's shoes was Pedro Carmona, president of Fedecámaras, Venezuela's chamber of commerce. In a December 2001 cable from the embassy in Caracas to the CIA, DIA, National Security Council, and other embassies in Bogota, Quito, La Paz, Lima, Mexico, Buenos Aires, Brasilia, and the U.S. Interests Section in Cuba, Ambassador Shapiro referred to

Pedro Carmona as "statesman-like" and "the right man for the right time in Venezuela."[13] In the months that followed, Carmona and fellow CTV leader Carlos Ortega took several trips to Washington accompanied by other prominent opposition leaders and NED grantees.[14] By the end of February 2002, Fedecámaras and the CTV, along with opposition-aligned political parties and social organizations, were calling for massive marches in the streets of Caracas.

On April 10, 2002, an NED-sponsored conference to "promote democracy" in Venezuela had been planned by grantee Consorcio Justicia. One of the headline speakers programmed for the conference was Pedro Carmona. But the conference, which was financed by Consorcio Justicia's $84,000 NED grant, never took place due to the strikes and protests occurring throughout Caracas that day.[15] In an increasingly tense situation, the private media channels aired a video segment showing a high-level general, Nestor Gonzalez Gonzalez, declaring rebellion and publicly calling for President Chávez to "step down." Later, it was revealed that General Gonzalez Gonzalez had prefabricated that media moment in order to prevent Chávez from attending an Organization of American States assembly meeting in Costa Rica, so that the president would remain in the country and the coup plan could be activated. General Gonzalez Gonzalez succeeded in his efforts, and on April 11, 2002, CTV, Fedecámaras, and NED-supported opposition parties held one of the largest rallies and marches Venezuela had ever seen.

About midday on April 11, the opposition march unlawfully altered its authorized route and millions began storming toward the presidential palace, Miraflores. A pro-Chávez rally occurring in front of Miraflores became alerted to the opposition's movements and the Presidential Guard was called out to ensure the two sides, now riled up, would not clash. Before the opposition marchers even reached the side of Miraflores where the pro-Chávez supporters were gathered, shots began ringing out from atop buildings surrounding the palace, and the first to fall were in the pro-Chávez crowd. Soon, innocent victims from both factions were hit, and before it was clear as to what was happening on the ground, images were broadcast on the private television channels with a voice-over blaming the Chávez supporters for the violence and declaring the resulting deaths and injuries the fault of President Chávez. Utilizing the manipulated images as justification, the military officers, who had already declared rebellion, together with opposition leaders stormed Miraflores and attempted to force President Chávez's resignation.

As a result of President Chávez's defiance, he was kidnapped and imprisoned in a nearby military base. The palace was taken over by opposition leaders and the state-owned television channel, which had broadcast a substantially different account of events than the private media, was shut down by force. Soon after, Pedro Carmona was sworn in as interim president, and in a sweeping first act, he issued a decree dissolving all of Venezuela's democratic institutions. The reading of the "Carmona Decree," as it was later referred to, was broadcast by the private media and endorsed by more than 395 Venezuelans present in the palace. In the meantime, pro-Chávez legislators, such as Tarek William Saab and other supporters, were brutally attacked and detained by the Caracas police force, under the control of opposition leader and mayor Alfredo Peña. The IRI had worked closely with Peña during 2001 to "shape his image" and NED-funded Liderazgo y Visión organization had received a $42,207 grant to work with the Caracas police force, several members of which were later charged with the homicides of pro-Chávez supporters killed during the events of April 11, 2002.[16]

In the course of events on coup day, multinational media mogul and close Bush family friend Gustavo Cisneros hosted Carmona, CTV head Carlos Ortega, and other opposition leaders and media owners at his Venevisión television headquarters for briefings and meetings. Also, several phone calls and visits were made between Otto Reich, Elliot Abrams, Ambassador Shapiro, and Pedro Carmona throughout the day. All of these contacts were verified later, but excused as merely "normal communications" during a time of heightened risk.

One of Ambassador Shapiro's first cables to Washington after the intense events of the day said: "Televised scenes of joy have marked the return of Petroleos de Venezuela (PDVSA) employees to their La Campiña headquarters building . . . PDVSA executives underline that the company should return to normal operations by early next week. Shipments are expected to resume today. PDVSA spokesperson stated publicly that no oil will be sent to Cuba."[17] Evidently, the primary preoccupation of the U.S.

government appeared to be its guaranteed oil flow. Venezuela is the fourth-largest exporter of oil in the world and the closest major oil supplier to the United States. Venezuela also owns eight oil refineries in the United States and the Citgo gas chain. Based on Ambassador Shapiro's reports of jubilance in the streets of Caracas and the "statesman-like" Carmona now in control of this strategically important country, President Bush's spokesman Ari Fleisher publicly announced the U.S. government's support for the "Carmona administration" and its condemnation of "Ex-President" Chávez for inciting the violence that forced him to "resign." The United States was one of the only countries in the world to rush to judgment on the muddled events of April 11 and openly recognize Pedro Carmona as a legitimate president. Considering that officials of the U.S. government had been prepping Mr. Carmona for this moment for months explained the immediate level of confidence they had in him.

The events of the following 48 hours drastically altered the old-school coup plan that had at first appeared successful. Millions of Chávez supporters filled the streets on April 13 demanding his return to office. At the same time, President Chávez was being held captive in another military base close to Maracay, Turiamo, where allegedly a plane was set to take him outside the country. The Presidential Guard, along with other factions of the military that had remained loyal to Chávez, swiftly forced Carmona and his advisors into detention and returned the palace grounds to the Chávez cabinet members, who then initiated the rescue of the constitutional president, Hugo Chávez.

Chávez's return to power in the early morning hours of April 14 came too late to stop the headlines and editorials in the *New York Times, Chicago Tribune,* and other international press which all praised the Venezuelan president's undemocratic ouster in the same tone as the Bush administration. The Venezuelan papers, though, had become remarkably silent. After multiple outbursts of joy and elation for Carmona's takeover and Chávez's forceful removal, the media was silent on April 13 and 14, imposing a blackout on information and news about developing events. Ambassador Shapiro's next cable to Washington carried the title, "Triumphant Return of Chávez" and referred to the Carmona decree as an "ill-fated declaration."

As calm and normalcy were established in Venezuela in the following days, the United States was forced to issue a statement recognizing the legitimacy of the Chávez government. But that did not stop the continued efforts to oust Chávez through other means. In April 2002, shortly after the failed coup, the U.S. Department of State issued a grant of $1 million in "special Venezuela funds" to NED. NED proceeded to distribute these extra funds to the very same groups that had just played key roles in the coup against President Chávez. Asamblea de Educación, whose president, Leonardo Carvajal, had been named education minister by Carmona, was given a new grant of $57,000. Fundación Momento de la Gente, whose director, Mercedes de Freitas, has tried her best to explain to NED that a coup never took place, was awarded $64,000. Asociación Civil Liderazgo y Visión, at the time directed by Oscar Garcia Mendoza, who not only published two congratulatory declarations for the Carmona government in the national newspapers on April 12 but also signed a civil society decree recognizing the legitimacy of Carmona as president, received $42,207. CEDICE, through NED core grantee CIPE, was awarded $116,525, despite the fact that its director, Rocio Guijarro, was one of the first signers and endorsers of the "ill-fated" Carmona Decree. And the International Republican Institute, which had issued a laudatory statement in favor of the coup and Carmona's takeover on April 12, was given $116,000 to continue its work with Primero Justicia, despite the fact that several of the parties' leaders had signed the Carmona Decree and one had even been named minister of finances under Carmona. The ACILS was given an additional $116,525 to finance the CTV, despite the union's visible participation in the coup.

The failure of the coup resonated uncomfortably with the U.S. government. The $1 million special grant from the State Department for NED projects in Venezuela clearly was not going to cover future efforts at regime change in Venezuela. Therefore, just a few months after the coup, the State Department ordered the placement of a USAID Office of Transition Initiatives (OTI) in Venezuela.

The concept of the OTI was established by USAID in 1994 "to respond to countries experiencing a significant and sometimes rapid political transition, which may or may not be accompanied by a social and/or economic crisis." The OTI "assesses, designs and implements programs that have characteristics of being fast, flexible, innovative, tangible, targeted, catalytic and overtly political, focusing on the root causes of the crisis."[18] OTIs have been used previously in Kosovo, Haiti, Indonesia, Peru, Guatemala, the Philippines, and Colombia, among other nations. USAID generally engages its OTIs to establish relationships with political organizations, media, and NGOs and to provide necessary funding and training to obtain desired results. OTIs often use contractors to provide additional support and administration of funds. The contractor sets up a parallel office, hires staff, establishes communications systems, and selects and monitors grantees. According to USAID, contractors are "critical to the success of OTI programs because they are expected to overcome the significant challenges posed by 'war torn' or otherwise unstable countries in which OTI operates."[19]

In Venezuela, the OTI set up shop in the U.S. embassy in Caracas in June 2002. From the beginning, the OTI program has been closely coordinated with the U.S. embassy. Indeed, the OTI program director reports directly to the U.S. ambassador. The OTI's initial budget in 2002 was $2,197,066—more than double that of NED's for just half a year. Soon after its founding in Venezuela, the OTI awarded Development Alternatives, Inc., a private U.S. consulting company, with a $10 million contract to establish and monitor a grant fund and program in "direct response to increasing political polarization in Venezuela."

II
The Strike

Development Alternatives Inc. (DAI) quickly moved to establish its office in the swanky El Rosal sector of Caracas, right down the road from the International Republican Institute's Venezuela headquarters. DAI also promptly complied with its contractual obligations and announced the creation of the Venezuela Construction of Confidence Initiative, or Venezuela: Iniciativa para la Construcción de Confianza (VICC). DAI claimed its purpose, along with the OTI, was to step in "to assist Venezuelans in fostering political conditions that would preclude violent conflict and systemic breakdown."[20]

Yet both DAI along with NED chose to fund many of those very same groups that had openly participated in and even led the coup against President Chávez. One of the first few grants DAI distributed in Venezuela under its VICC program was for the purpose of "promoting social dialogue and citizen formation" using mass media. The project involved the creation of television and radio commercials to promote "democratic and modern values, rupturing the patterns of paternalism and populism."[21] The project also assured the collaboration of Fedecámaras president Carlos Fernandez. After the failed April coup, Carmona had escaped from his home arrest and fled the country, obtaining political asylum in neighboring Colombia. Fernandez was left holding the reigns of the nation's most powerful business association, and he continued Carmona's efforts to seek premature removal of President Chávez from office.

The particular timing of this DAI project focused on radio and television commercials was key. On December 2, 2002, Fedecámaras, the CTV, and the opposition parties, now known as the Coordinadora Democrática (Democratic Coordinator), launched a national general strike intended to destabilize Venezuela's economy and force President Chávez to resign. In support of the opposition's objectives, the private media symbolically joined the strike by suspending all regular programming and commercials and donating one hundred percent of on-air space to the opposition. The Coordinadora Democrática, with the help of Venezuela's top public relations firms, produced some of the most highly crafted anti-Chávez commercials Venezuelans had ever seen. These commercials, broadcast often ten at a time in between coverage of opposition marches, speeches, and interviews, contained varying messages on Chávez's failures, alleged human rights abuses, and the overall political crisis and poor state of the nation. Some of the commercials exploited images of children singing and stamping red handprints, symbolizing blood, on walls, with messages about the "future of the nation," the "safety of children," and the "need for a new Venezuela." The DAI radio and television commercial project in collaboration with Carlos Fernandez began on December 9, 2002, just seven days after the strike and the propaganda war had begun.

After the failure of the coup in April and the installation of the OTI in June and later the initiation of the DAI Venezuela initiative in August, the

Coordindora Democrática (CD) emerged. Strange timing, familiar name. Born in the likes of the Coordinadora Democrática Nicaragüense, the Venezuelan CD was composed of Fedecámaras, the CTV, numerous civil society organizations, and about ten different political parties, many of which were ongoing NED recipients. Instead of reflecting on the incidents of April 11–14 that had paralyzed the nation and altered Venezuela's future, the CD immediately began working on the next phase. Although the Organization of American States had sent a delegation to help negotiate a solution, led by Secretary General Cesar Gaviria, the opposition was set on just one way out of the crisis: Chávez's removal from the presidency.

In October 2002, dissident military officers, many of whom had played key roles in the coup, declared a state of rebellion and claimed a plaza in the wealthy eastern section of Caracas, declaring it a "liberated zone." The CD and the private media, which publicly supported the military rebellion, utilized the growing chaos as a platform to call for a national strike in early December. On the second day of the strike, Secretary of State Colin Powell met in Bogotá with interim coup president Pedro Carmona, who, according to Colombian newspapers, had met frequently with the U.S. ambassador in that nation, Ann Patterson.[22] Considering that Carmona was still in contact with his Fedecámaras counterpart and that the business association was the principal instigator and promoter of the strike, the meeting between the U.S. foreign minister and an exiled coup leader playing an ongoing role in destabilizing a democratic nation seemed out of place. But apparently such behavior was the norm for the U.S. government. In fact, Pedro Carmona had made frequent, uninhibited trips to the United States right after the coup in April, and it was outrage from the international community that later led the State Department to revoke his tourist visa.[23]

The CD-led strike lasted 64 days, into February 2003. The economic damage exceeded billions of dollars. The strike, which in many areas was more of a lockout, since business owners shut down companies, therefore forcing employees to not work, focused on the oil industry, Venezuela's lifeline and principal source of income. A faction of workers in PDVSA, primarily management employees led by Juan Fernandez, formed an entity known as Gente de Petroleo that became a part of the CD. The managers and other workers in PDVSA who joined the strike not only violated their own contracts but also made it impossible for supplemental workers to access codes and authorized areas in order to run the refineries and other industry operations. A little known but strategically important venture between a U.S. company with CIA ties, Science Applications International Corporation (SAIC), and PDVSA, called INTESA, played a key role in crippling Venezuela's oil industry.

INTESA, the information and technology enterprise that was formed to run all electronic operations at PDVSA and to update many of the older, analog systems to high-tech, not only promptly joined the strike but also sabotaged essential equipment and networks necessary to run the industry. From remote locations, INTESA employees altered access codes and programming, making it impossible for remaining PDVSA workers to run computers, machines, and refinery equipment. As a result, oil production was brought to a halt, and the losses were devastating. Not only were common Venezuelans denied gas and oil, but also Venezuela's contracts with international partners were severely threatened. Venezuela had to purchase petroleum from other nations in order to minimally cover its contractual obligations. Lines to get gasoline in some parts of Venezuela were more than five miles long. As the strike continued through the end of December, many taxi drivers and car owners spent Christmas Eve staked out in their cars on line, waiting for a ration of gasoline. Millions of citizens with no electric appliances were forced to cook with wood fires, even in the middle of Caracas, throughout the 64-day strike.

INTES's majority shareholder, SAIC, which owned 60 percent of the company (to PDVS's 40 percent), is a major contractor for the U.S. government. With former chiefs of staff, ex-CIA agents, and high-level government employees making up its board of directors, SAIC is closely linked to the U.S. government, and not just through contracts. Furthermore, cables sent from the U.S. embassy during the negotiations between PDVSA and SAIC regarding the formation of INTESA stated that the joint venture was of "critical importance" to the United States.

PDVS's president, Ali Rodriguez, tried to amicably resolve the situation with INTESA during the strike by informing the company of its contractual obligations and to continue provision of services. Once INTES's management refused to comply with PDVSA, Rodriguez requested they turn over access codes to equipment so that PDVSA employees could operate the machinery and get the industry off the ground. This exchange went on for several weeks. INTESA continued to refuse cooperation with PDVSA and eventually PDVSA employees had to enter INTESA headquarters and seize operating equipment in order to return Venezuela's oil industry to a functional state.

At the same time, the White House called for early elections in Venezuela in order to end the political crisis. The U.S. government, which had tacitly supported the coup against Chávez, now supported an unconstitutional solution in Venezuela. The Venezuelan constitution has no provision for calling early elections when political crises arise. Nevertheless, on December 13, 2002, the White House issued a statement declaring, "The United States is convinced that the only peaceful and politically viable path to moving out of the crisis is through the holding of early elections."[24] On that same day, Richard Boucher, spokesperson for the State Department, made a revealing comment in a daily press briefing, stating, "An early election, we think, is the kind of solution that's needed. And I guess you could say that's our objective."[25] Clearly, the U.S. had an objective in mind: undermine the Venezuelan constitution by calling for unconstitutional elections in order to push Chávez out of office under the guise of a democratic electoral process. After all, who then could deny that elections are democratic?

During that same period, the Department of Defense was sending bogus intelligence reports to Washington to paint a pariah image of President Chávez. One December 2002 cable falsely claimed that Chávez had "ordered the destruction of television stations Globovisión, Televen, Canal Dos and possibly other media outlets. These attacks are scheduled to take place on the evening of 12 December." President Chávez had never ordered such attacks, nor were these stations ever destroyed. Those very same television outlets were broadcasting 24-hour-a-day, uncensored anti-Chávez messages that in many cases were violent and aggressive and the state had taken no action to inhibit freedom of expression. But those receiving the information up in Washington did not know that the report was false. The same report discussed "Cuban troops and Revolutionary Armed Forces of Colombia guerrillas in Venezuela to support Chávez," clearly intending to link the Venezuelan leader to Colombian terrorists, opening the door to international intervention.[26]

In a strange coincidence of time, place, and facts, a new entity was born in Venezuela. As SAIC was pushed out of PDVSA, losing its grip on the most important oil industry in the Western Hemisphere, Súmate, a technologically advanced, elections-focused nonprofit run by opposition-aligned wealthy Venezuelans, was established.[27] Súmate's premiere came at the tail end of the strike, which had failed in its objective of ousting Chávez, but had succeeded in making Venezuelans' lives miserable through economic devastation. The opposition was heeding the "early elections" calls of the U.S., but the government rightfully refused to permit such an unconstitutional gesture. Súmate offered an alternative to a desperate opposition movement and an eager U.S. government: a referendum.

Venezuela's 1999 constitution includes a provision in Article 72 to solicit a recall referendum on any public official's mandate after the halfway point of the term has been met. The referendum must be solicited by 20 percent of the electorate and then a greater number of voters that elected the official must vote to recall, and those recall votes must have a majority over those voting to keep the official in office. It is a complex process. Unfortunately, Súmate, riding the high of its clever proposal, forgot to read the content of Article 72 and in early February 2003 began a signature drive to petition for a referendum. Claiming they had collected millions of signatures in support of a recall referendum on President Chávez's mandate, Súmate demanded the government immediately convene an election. Súmate's demands fell short of the ears of the Venezuelan government, since the halfway point of President Chávez's term had not yet been met, but another government heard them loud and clear. The U.S. awarded Súmate for their brave and bold actions handsomely. Both NED and USAID granted Súmate funds to continue their fight for the referendum.[28] Súmate, in the likes of Vía Cívica in Nicaragua, was held out to be a neutral organization devoted to electoral education, but Súmate's own website clearly stated the organization's objective was to "promote a recall referendum against President Chávez."[29] Furthermore, Súmate's vice president and treasurer, Maria Corina Machado, had signed the infamous Carmona Decree during the coup, indicating a clear anti-Chávez bias and undemocratic tendencies. And Súmate's president, Alejandro Plaz, was the director of the Andean office of McKinsey & Company, a consulting firm notoriously linked to the CIA.

III
The Referendum

For fiscal year 2003, USAID's OTI requested $5,074,000 for its Venezuela operations. NED gave out more than $1 million to its Venezuela grantees and counterparts, many of which were the very same organizations that had just spearheaded the illegal 64-day strike that devastated Venezuela's economy. DAI also continued to dish out grants to projects falling within its VICC program. After the failure of the strike, it became clear that the opposition needed to consolidate and focus on an electoral solution that would appear legitimate in the eyes of the world. The constitution opened the doors to the possibility of the recall referendum, and in May 2003, after more than nine months of brokering by the OAS, the opposition agreed to seek a "peaceful and constitutional" solution to the crisis. Since early elections were unconstitutional, the referendum would be the only possible way of prematurely removing President Chávez from office.

Súmate immediately spearheaded a campaign to force the government to accept the signatures it had gathered back in February 2003. The private media and international press, encouraged by the U.S. government, supported this demand. Yet Venezuela's National Electoral Council (CNE), an autonomous governmental body, announced that it would not accept signatures gathered, a clear violation of referendum requirements. The CNE then released a clear set of guidelines that would regulate the referendum process. A date was set in late November for a petition drive to be held in support of a recall referendum. If the required 20 percent of voters' signatures, approximately 2.4 million, were obtained, then a recall referendum on President Chávez's mandate would be held.

Súmate promptly launched a massive media and propaganda campaign in support of the petition drive, referred to as the "Reafirmazo." Utilizing NED and USAID funding, Súmate mass-produced anti-Chávez and pro-referendum materials that were distributed nationwide. The organization also produced little blue cards which affirmed that a voter had signed the petition for a recall referendum. The cards were distributed at petition drive tables and voters were told to turn them in to employers, or else face termination. In fall 2003, the OTI requested an additional $6,345,000 for use in

Venezuela during 2004. USAID also gave the International Republican Institute and the National Democratic Institute more than $2 million for "strengthening political parties" and "promoting electoral processes" in Venezuela during 2003–4. NDI's grant specifically mentioned collaborations with Súmate.

Right around the time of the Reafirmazo, the U.S. launched another attack against the Chávez government, this time claiming Venezuela was harboring terrorist training camps and was collaborating with the Colombian FARC and ELN, both groups on the U.S. list of international terrorist organizations. An October article in *U.S. News and World Report* by Linda Robinson, titled "Terror Close to Home," claimed that Al Qaeda, FARC, and ELN terrorists had training camps scattered throughout Venezuela. These allegations were based on comments by an "anonymous U.S. official" and were never substantiated. Around the same time, the Department of Defense circulated an "Intelligence Assessment" alleging Chávez had supplied $1 million to the FARC and ELN in Colombia and was building armed guerrilla groups to defend his "revolution." The report cited as its intelligence sources, El Universal, El Nacional, and Globovisión television station in Venezuela, all staunchly anti-Chávez media. No other sources were provided in the report to substantiate the claim.[30]

Despite these international pressures, the signature collection period went smoothly, but the CNE later determined only 1.9 million signatures valid, while another nearly 1 million were set aside and questioned for fraud. The opposition reacted to the news with violence. In February 2004, newly formed extremist factions in the Coordinadora Democrática launched the "Guarimba," a plan allegedly formed by Cuban-Venezuelan Robert Alonso. The Guarimba called for right-wing forces to engage in widespread civil disobedience and violence in the streets of Caracas and other metropolitan areas, provoking repressive reactions from state forces that would then justify cries of human rights violations and lack of constitutional order. The Guarimba lasted from February 27 to March 1, 2004, and during that period numerous Venezuelan citizens were injured and arrested for violations of law. The opposition-controlled media in Venezuela quickly broadcast to the world a prepared version of events that cited the government as the "repressor" and portrayed claims of those arrested during that period for breaking the law as "victims of torture and unlawful arrest." The Guarimba starkly resembled the Chileanization strategy applied in Chile and Nicaragua, using similar tactics and provoking identical results.

As a result of the violence and instability again caused by the opposition, the Venezuelan government agreed to allow those signatures that had appeared fraudulent to be "reaffirmed" by the signers over a four-day period regulated by the CNE. As such, the opposition was provided with a second opportunity to legitimately obtain the necessary 2.4 million signatures needed to hold the recall referendum. The signature repair period, "reparo," as it was known, was held at the end of May 2004. The Carter Center and the OAS provided international observation.

The opposition obtained the necessary 2.4 million signatures by an additional 100,000 obtained in the repair process, and the referendum date was set for August 15, 2004. About five days after the announcement confirming the referendum, the opposition released an alternative plan for a transitional post-Chávez government. Titled "Plan Consensus," the project appeared as the first attempt by the opposition to offer Venezuelans something beyond a strict "get Chávez out of office" position. The opposition had been highly criticized internationally for having no concrete plans, no viable candidates to oppose Chávez, and no platform on which to campaign. The Plan Consensus appeared to be the magic solution. But Plan Consensus's polished offerings were not born independently from the opposition. They were the result of an NED grant to CIPE-CEDICE in 2003, combined with USAID funding that had gone through DAI to several opposition groups, including Liderazgo y Visión and Queremos Eligir.

Additionally, both IRI and NDI had played roles and had financed the crafting of this alternative agenda. It was the goal of the U.S. to win the referendum and install a transitional government that would work best in its interests. As such, the referendum campaign, via Súmate and the CD, and the alternative agenda, via NED and USAID grantees, were financed and overseen by U.S. government agents.[31] NED chose CEDICE as the principal drafter of an agenda for a transitional government despite the fact that CEDICE's president, Rocio Guijarro, was one of the initial signers of the Carmona Decree and was chosen by Carmona to represent NGOs at his swearing-in ceremony. CEDICE also happened to be one of the most fer-

vently outspoken anti-Chávez groups in Venezuela, whose leaders attempted several times to convince NED program director Christopher Sabatini
that a coup d'état did not take place on April 11, 2002; rather it was a popular uprising against a "dictator."[32]

Despite the millions of dollars invested in the opposition to Chávez, on
August 15, 2004, more than 59 percent of Venezuelans voted to ratify his
mandate and keep him in office.[33] Even though both the Carter Center and
the OAS certified the official CNE referendum results, the opposition, led
by Súmate, cried fraud. Súmate claimed it had conducted an exit poll with
the U.S. polling firm Penn, Schoen & Berland, previously used in electoral
interventions in Nicaragua, Panamá, and Yugoslavia, that showed the exact
opposite results—the vote to recall Chávez had exceeded 59 percent.[34] An
exit poll by the extreme right-wing anti-Chávez party and IRI counterpart,
Primero Justicia, also showed that result. All other exit polls conducted by
international firms and independent observers were in line with the official
CNE results. However, Súmate and the CD claimed the vote had been
fraudulently calculated and refused to recognize the results.

After the Storm

Miami, Florida, has become a haven for self-exiled Venezuelans seeking new
ways of ousting President Chávez from his democratically elected office. In
early October 2004, Guarimba founder Robert Alonso surfaced in Miami
after a warrant had been issued for his arrest in Venezuela in connection
with the approximately 80 Colombian paramilitaries found on his farm outside of Caracas in May 2004. Also, former Venezuelan president Carlos
Andrés Pérez has taken root in Miami and has played a key role in destabilization efforts to remove Chávez from office. From his home in Miami in
July 2004, CAP declared to *El Nacional* newspaper that Chávez deserved
to "die like a dog" and that "violence is the only way to remove him."[35]

Several other ex-military officers known to have participated in the coup
have appeared in Miami alongside Carlos Fernandez, the former
Fedecámaras president, and Carlos Ortega, former CTV president, who
had obtained political asylum in Costa Rica, but later lost it once he clan-

destinely returned to Venezuela and appeared on television in a pre-referendum rally. He was arrested in 2005 at a Caracas bingo hall, wearing a Pancho Villa mustache disguise, but soon after escaped prison with the complicity of several guards. He remains a fugitive-at-large. The Venezuelan government had issued arrest warrants for both Fernandez and Ortega in 2003 for their leadership of the illegal 64-day strike that caused billions of dollars in losses to Venezuela's economy. The Venezuelan government also has pending extradition requests with the U.S. government for two military officers, German Rodolfo Varela and Jose Antonio Colina, alleged to be the masterminds behind the bombings of the Colombian and Spanish embassies in Caracas in fall 2003. The officers have requested political asylum and have pending cases before immigration judges in Miami.

There have also been reports of anti-Chávez terrorist training camps in Miami, run by self-exiled Venezuelan extremists and former military officers who have joined forces with Miami's notorious anti-Castro community. Despite requests from the Venezuelan government for the U.S. government to investigate these camps, no action has been taken. And Cuba-Venezuelan terrorist Luis Posada Carriles, responsible for planning the bombing of a Cuban airliner in 1976, killing all 73 passengers on board, was released from an immigration detention center in Texas after being granted his freedom by the U.S. court system. Venezuela requested his extradition in May 2005, but has received no response from the U.S. government. Posada Carriles, who escaped from prison in Venezuela in 1987, and remains a fugitive from justice, allegedly has been plotting with other Venezuelan and Cuban extremists in Miami to assassinate President Chávez and incite violence and instability in the South American nation. The U.S. government has remained silent on the issue.

1

Washington's Ongoing War on Venezuela:
An Overview

In 2006, Hugo Chávez Frías was up for reelection. The opposition coalition, known as UNITY, agreed on a single candidate, Manuel Rosales, governor of the state of Zulia in western Venezuela, home to the nation's prosperous and developed oil industry. Rosales was backed by a coalition of political parties, civil society organizations, labor unions, business associations, mass media, and the hierarchy of the Catholic Church that executed the coup d'état against Chávez in April 2002. He ran on an empty ticket. His campaign promised to eradicate poverty by supplying citizens with "debit cards" to charge away on in good ol' American style, and the colors of his paraphernalia tell where his loyalties stood: red, white, and blue.

The parties, groups, and media that oppose Chávez are amply funded by U.S. entities such as the National Endowment for Democracy and the United States Agency for International Development (USAID), in an effort to remove Chávez prematurely from power. All those attempts have failed, yet the intervention has grown. Chávez won the 2006 presidential elections by a landslide victory, 64 percent of a vote that had the highest level of participation by the Venezuelan electorate in the history of the nation. Nevertheless, U.S. interference in that campaign was noteworthy, and efforts to discredit Chávez as a legitimate president of a democratic nation continue in full force. Despite four solid elections under his hat (1998, 1999, 2004 and 2006), each garnering a larger majority of votes and voter participation, Washington continues to intensify its efforts to impede Venezuela's progress and development of its own unique political and economic system.

The information about the actions—many of them illegal—of the U.S.
government in Venezuela, through the Central Intelligence Agency, the
State Department, and other entities operating within Venezuela and strategically from inside Washington, is voluminous and overwhelming. Since the
publication of *The Chávez Code* in early 2005, we have witnessed a serious
and scary shift in U.S. policy toward Venezuela. Three major fronts of attack
have been launched and are rapidly taking form: the financial, the diplomatic, and the military. These have become the battlefields for which a new
form of war—asymmetric warfare—is being waged on the Venezuelan people and their government. This is a war with no clear lines, a war without
frontiers, and a war, it seems, with no end.

The Financial Front

The financial front commenced in 2001, when the National Endowment for
Democracy quadrupled its annual funding to anti-Chávez groups that later
used those same funds to plan and execute the coup against Chávez. The
funds, at that time around one million dollars annually, were conveniently
increased just a mere two weeks after the coup, and were disbursed to the
same groups that had just participated in the overthrow of Venezuela's democratically elected government. The State Department issued a $1 million
special fund to the National Endowment for Democracy for its Venezuela
projects, and instead of restricting funding to organizations that had just led
a coup—a total violation of democratic principles—the money was quickly
distributed among them.

Despite documentation from the National Endowment for Democracy
that disproves compliance with its "democratic" mission, NED has augmented its funding annually to opposition groups in Venezuela. President
Bush requested Congress to double NED's budget for its work in Venezuela
during 2005–6, and again for fiscal year 2007–08.[1]

Almost simultaneously, funding has grown for the United States Agency
for International Development (USAID) and its Office for Transition
Initiatives (OTI) which operates out of the U.S. embassy in Caracas and contracts a private U.S. corporation, Development Alternatives, Inc., to admin-

ister its more than $10 million budget. Instead of the $5 million it was receiving annually from the State Department back in 2002, the latest figures show an increase to $7 million for fiscal year 2005, and spokespersons for the Department of State have indicated a desire to raise these funds even more. These millions in U.S. taxpayer dollars play a significant role in the financial role the Bush administration has laid out against Venezuela. The Office for Transition Initiatives, which opened in June 2002, just two months after the coup against President Chávez, was set to be an "in and out" operation completed within two years. The OTI has been extended indefinitely in Venezuela and its offices have grown. Development Alternatives, Inc., which opened an affiliate branch in the fancy El Rosal district of Caracas—the nation's equivalent of Wall Street—has become a permanent fixture on the scene, operating like a CIA front company that supplies millions of U.S. taxpayer dollars to anti-Chávez groups in Venezuela.

USAID's intervention in Venezuela has also gone nationwide, and the U.S. ambassador from August 2004 to August 2007, William Brownfield, took the lead in disguising the entity as a generous, kindhearted source of donations to community-based groups and projects. Ambassador Brownfield has engaged in a tactful public relations campaign to refurbish the agency's image. His publicity stunts resulted in tomato and egg throwing by Chávez supporters in the communities the ambassador attempted to buy with USAID donations.

A new angle on this financial front came with the launching of the first American Corners in Latin America, all of which are in Venezuela. The American Corners program first began in Russia in the 1990s and expanded in 2002 to other parts of Eastern Europe where U.S. involvement and interests were growing, such as Uzbekistan, Kyrgyzstan, Bulgaria, Poland, Turkey, and Central and East Asian nations including Oman, Bangladesh, Pakistan, Indonesia, and Afghanistan. According to the US embassy's website, American Corners are "partnerships between the Public Affairs sections of U.S. embassies and host institutions. They provide access to current and reliable information about the U.S. via book collections, the internet, and through local programming to the general public." [2]

But what really are these so-called Corners? The U.S. refers to them as "satellite consulates," a concept that violates the principles of international diplomacy law.[3] In Venezuela, the U.S. embassy has set up four of these "Corners" in the cities of Margarita, Barquisimeto, Maturín, and Lecherías, Anzoátegui State—all without authorization from the Foreign Ministry. By hiding the "satellite consulates" inside lawyers' associations and opposition municipal mayors' offices, the State Department probably thought they would be protected from inquiry. And these are not regular consulates— they do not provide any services to American citizens in those parts of the country; rather, they are spaces where Venezuelans can gather to make contacts with U.S. representatives and obtain ideological materials that perpetuate the U.S. model of neoliberalism and capitalism.

The register is ringing on the financial front, as more and more "projects" are launched that serve as façades for new and inventive ways to filter the millions into the Venezuelan opposition. With the assignment of a new special CIA mission to oversee and intensify intelligence activities and collection of "precise" information in Venezuela and Cuba, announced by the Director of National Intelligence on August 18, 2006, we can be assured that the dollars flowing into counterrevolutionary groups in Venezuela will increase dramatically over the next few months.

These issues will be discussed in detail in the following chapters.

The Diplomatic Front

The U.S. government has spent the last two years imposing every possible unilateral sanction on the Venezuelan government that it could conjure up. Despite State Department documents authored by Ambassador William Brownfield that verify Venezuela's successful counter-narcotics measures, in September 2005 the Bush administration issued a report indicating that Venezuela had "failed demonstrably" to prevent drug shipments to the United States.[4] In the same breath, the statement released by the White House on the subject indicated that "the President is also determined to maintain U.S. programs that aid Venezuela's democratic institutions, establish selected community development projects, and strengthen Venezuela's political party system," which means not cutting funding from NED and USAID to opposition groups in Venezuela.[5] It's a kind of half sanction. The

Congress of the United States has not been so wishy-washy on the subject. Dan Burton, chairman of the House of Representatives Committee on International Relations, pushed for passage of Resolution 400, which condemns Venezuela's alleged "failure to cooperate with the war on drugs" and falsely accuses the Venezuelan government of actually "creating fertile ground for criminal drug trafficking organizations," among other things.[6]

But a classified report sent from the U.S. embassy in Caracas and signed by the ambassador, dated January 2005, contradicts the Congress and the executive branch: "The Venezuelan government cooperates on counter-narcotics matters, limited at times by a lack of resources and political will. Cocaine seizures during the first six months of 2004 equaled the amount seized in Venezuela during all of 2003, thanks in large part to two multi-ton seizures made by Venezuelan task forces working closely with USG and UK law enforcement. The government also carried out some 400 cocaine and heroin seizures during the first half of the year. The GOV has extradited a number of drug traffickers to the U.S."[7] Clearly, this document demonstrates Venezuela's enhanced and successful efforts to cooperate with the drug war, and it indicates that the official and public statements made by U.S. government officials are merely aimed at manipulating public opinion on Venezuela. Nevertheless, the White House has maintained classification of Venezuela as a nation "complicit with drug-trafficking" since 2005, ratifying this stigmatization during 2006 and again in 2007.

Drugs are just one example of how the Bush administration has been fabricating evidence in the court of public opinion to justify its goal of regime change in Venezuela. Other sanctions include economic blockades for allegedly "not cooperating with regulations against trafficking in persons," also issued in early 2005, and the recent ban on arms sales to Venezuela for supposedly "not cooperating with the war on terrorism." This is the latest hostile and dangerous strategy Washington is employing against Venezuela.

At the same time, the Untied States has launched an international campaign to build what Secretary of State Condoleezza Rice referred to as "a united international front against Venezuela."[8] The goal of this "united front" would be to garner support from other nations around the world to take multilateral action against "the growing danger of Hugo Chávez."[9] So far, the mission has failed, but the efforts continue to increase to achieve this goal.

The Military Front

The third angle of attack against the Venezuelan government originating from Washington is by far the most dangerous and complicated. The military front involves more than just the recent buildup of U.S. military troops, operations, and equipment in the Caribbean Basin and the Andean Region surrounding Venezuela. It also employs the use of psychological operations (psyops)—psychological warfare—a strategy referred to in the 2003 version of the Department of Defense's Doctrine on Psychological Operations as "one of the most powerful weapons the Pentagon has today."[10] The major psyops campaign against Venezuela attempts to link President Chávez to terrorism and nuclear ambitions, as well as classifying his government as a "dictatorship". This will be fully analyzed in chapter 8.

Asymmetric warfare is the new terminology used to describe what in the past century was referred to as "low-intensity conflicts." Asymmetric war, or fourth-generation irregular war, is known as the "war as a whole" or "war of all people." This type of war may be military or nonmilitary, lethal or nonlethal, or a mix of everything—all rules apply and there are no rules at all. It can involve everything from diplomatic strategies (trying to build international coalitions against the nation-state), financial backing of opposition movements, direct military threats, and electoral interventions. In sum, all the tactics the U.S. government is employing today against Venezuela. This concept will be addressed and expanded on in chapter 7.

Finally, the other major aspect of the military front involves espionage and CIA sabotage endeavors. Even though the CIA is technically a civilian outlet in the intelligence community, the recent restructuring of all intelligence agencies and the creation of the Directorate of National Intelligence in early 2005, headed by John Negroponte, has moved the CIA into a realm that directly operates in connection with the Defense Intelligence Agency and other military intelligence divisions. Furthermore, the May 30, 2006, appointment of U.S. Air Force General Michael V. Hayden as CIA director indicated the growing power of the military over all intelligence operations. Therefore, throughout this book, the CIA will be viewed as an appendage to the giant military intelligence complex that operates internationally to execute the U.S. agenda of domination and global economic control. Acts of espionage and sabotage will be reviewed in chapter 9.

2

Condi Rice's Negative Force

"I think that we have to view at this point the government of Venezuela as a negative force in the region." Those were Condoleezza Rice's first statements on Venezuela during her confirmation hearings before the Senate Foreign Relations Committee on January 18, 2005. "We can, I think, work with others to expose that, and say to President Chávez that this kind of behavior is really not acceptable in this Hemisphere that is trying to make its way toward a stable democratic future," she continued, setting the stage for U.S.-Venezuela relations for the months to come.[1]

This new form of so-called diplomacy raised the stakes on U.S. policy toward Venezuela. Now, instead of working behind the scenes, focusing on financing and building a solid opposition movement within Venezuela, a strategy that had failed embarrassingly, Washington had taken a decisive stance. Chávez would be classified as a "threat to democracy" and a "destabilizing, negative force" in the hemisphere. This rhetoric, which emanated from the new Secretary of State Rice during her opening statements at the Senate hearings, would be repeated throughout the following weeks and months in the U.S. press and from other notable spokespersons of the U.S. government.

The CIA Speaks

Barely one month later, then-director of the CIA Porter J. Goss labeled Venezuela as a "flashpoint" country during 2005. Addressing the Senate

Select Committee on Intelligence on February 16, 2005, Goss declared, "In Venezuela, Chávez is consolidating his power by using technically legal tactics to target his opponents and meddling in the region, supported by Castro."[2] The term "technically legal tactics" implies that Chávez really isn't doing anything wrong, but the CIA considers him a threat anyway. Though these statements could be taken at face value to merely indicate the expected CIA attention given to an emerging combative leadership in Venezuela, Goss's background as a CIA operative in Latin America in the 1960s, alongside many of the die-hard anti-Castro agents and terrorists, implies otherwise. Just months later, Goss commented about his "eagerness to reopen stations" in Latin America, so the agency is prepared when conflicts arise in "otherwise quiet areas."[3]

Goss also led in the creation of the National Clandestine Service (NCS), a new intelligence entity overseen by the CIA director that coordinates and supervises activities of "human intelligence" (HUMINT) abroad. The NCS, run by a high-level CIA operative known only by the alias "José," opened the doors for an expansion of nearly 50 percent of agency operatives around the world. Furthermore, during his brief reign at the CIA, Goss implemented plans to additionally expand the CIA's spying and analytical operations overseas, moving agency officers and analysts out of embassies and placing them under cover.[4]

A little more than one year later, this desire has become a reality. In August 2006, Director of National Intelligence John Negroponte launched a new special CIA mission manager to oversee, coordinate, and improve intelligence operations in Venezuela and Cuba. Negroponte, who coordinates the entire intelligence community in the United States and reports directly to President George W. Bush, named CIA veteran J. Patrick Maher as acting mission manager of this new important division. According to a press release from the Directorate of National Intelligence, "Maher will be responsible for integrating collection and analysis on Cuba and Venezuela across the Intelligence Community, identifying and filling gaps in intelligence, and ensuring the implementation of strategies, among other duties." Negroponte indicated that "such efforts are critical today, as policymakers have increasingly focused on the challenges that Cuba and Venezuela pose to American foreign policy." The new CIA mission manager for Cuba and

Venezuela will "be responsible for ensuring that policymakers have a full range of timely and accurate intelligence on which to base their decisions." This implies a further increase in actual ground agents and field officers in both nations. J. Patrick Maher is a seasoned CIA agent who joined the agency in 1974, after a two-year stint with the Peace Corps. His work was centered throughout Latin America, where he was based for more than thirty years.[5] In November 2006, veteran CIA officer and Cold War specialist Norman A. Bailey was assigned to take over the lead of this special CIA mission.

The only other nations assigned such missions, recommended by the Weapons of Mass Destruction Commission of the Directorate for National Intelligence, are Iran and North Korea. Such a designation demonstrates Washington's move to classify Venezuela as part of the so-called Axis of Evil.

And the steps to inch Venezuela closer to this designation were clear in early 2005, and even years before. A classified as "SECRET" cable from the U.S. embassy to the Department of State, CIA, and Defense Intelligence Agency dated April 2003 claimed that Venezuela was harboring different terrorist groups. The document, apparently a questionnaire on terrorism activities sent out to U.S. embassies around the world, was completed by then-ambassador Charles Shapiro, who indicated that in Venezuela, three local terrorist groups exist, the Jirajaras, the Coordinador Simon Bolivar, and the Frente Bolivariano de Venezuela. The secret document goes on to state that these groups have carried out attacks in the "capital or in areas where U.S. diplomatic facilities are located" and that such attacks have been "lethal." The cable also submits that the following "foreign terrorist groups" have a presence in the country: FARC, ELN, HIZBALLAH, ETA, AUC, and ASBAT AL-ANSAR, and, the document alleges, they receive "operational and financial support" within Venezuela.[6]

The Jirajaras represent an indigenous culture from the western part of Venezuela. In the 1960s, a rebel group existed under this name, but has absolutely no presence today in national politics. The Coordinadora Simon Bolivar is one of the oldest community grassroots organizations in the country, based in the 23 de Enero neighborhood in Caracas. The Coordinadora has done exemplary community-based work during decades and has served as a foundation for many of the cooperatives and social organizations that have been formed over the past few years under the new social programs of the Venezuelan government. They are clearly not a terrorist organization. The Frente Bolivariano de Venezuela, as cited by Shapiro in the cable, is an unknown entity. A Frente Bolivariano de Liberación does exist, but that is not the group named in the document.

But these groups are not the cause of concern. The alarming aspect of the document is the implication that Venezuela is a refuge for Middle Eastern terrorist groups that receive "operational and financial support" from the Venezuelan government or its supporters. Such statements are unfounded and unsubstantiated, and have been disproved on numerous occasions by the Venezuelan government and its allies. However, this information has served as a basis for the U.S. government to increase its claims that Venezuela is a nation linked to terrorism.

Roger Noriega, former Assistant Secretary for Western Hemisphere Affairs, confirmed this agenda when he stated before the Senate Foreign Relations Committee on March 2, 2005, that "Venezuela has the resources it needs for its own development, but we are concerned that President Hugo Chávez's very personal agenda may undermine democratic institutions at home and among his neighbors. Despite our efforts to establish a normal working relationship with his government, Hugo Chávez continues to define himself in opposition to the United States. His efforts to concentrate power at home, his suspect relationship with destabilizing forces in the region, and his plans for arms purchases are causes of major concern to the Bush Administration. We will support democratic elements in Venezuela so that they can continue to maintain the political space to which they are entitled, and we will increase awareness among Venezuela's neighbors of President Chávez's destabilizing acts with the expectation that they will join us in defending regional stability, security and prosperity."[7]

The cynicism of Noriega's statement overshadows any inkling of goodwill. To attempt to claim that the United States has made "efforts to establish a normal working relationship" with the Venezuelan government insults the intelligence of the international community and the substantial evidence that unquestionably documents the U.S. government's support of the April 2002 coup d'état against President Chávez, its multimillion-dollar financing of anti-Chávez groups, and its daily and unwavering hostile rhetoric. But more important, Noriega lays out the three major themes of misinformation that his government has been seeping into news media and public opinion ever since: Chávez is authoritarian/dictatorial; Chávez is a destabilizing force in the region; and Chávez has links with terrorism.

What to Do About Venezuela

By far, the most substantial and important document that lays out U.S. strategies for regime change and direct intervention is the report commissioned by the U.S. government, published by the Center for Security Policy, an ultra-right think tank in Washington. The text, titled "What to Do About Venezuela,"[8] is a blueprint for policy on Venezuela and is similar in content to the Project for a New American Century's plan for war in Iraq and its strategy for dominating the world's energy reserves.[9] Due to its obvious impact on U.S. foreign policy on Venezuela since publication in May 2005, the report deserves special attention.

"What to Do About Venezuela," authored by the Center for Security Policy's Vice President for Information Operations J. Michael Waller, is based on the premise that Chávez is a dictator who consorts with terrorists and threatens American interests, and therefore must be removed from power as soon as possible. The opening paragraphs of the report summarize: "Nowhere is the lack of a U.S. strategic approach to the Western Hemisphere more evident than in the unchecked rise of a self-absorbed, unstable strongman in Venezuela, Hugo Chávez, who has made common cause with terrorists and the regimes that support them, and has developed a revolutionary ideology that has begun to plunge the Americas again into violence and chaos. It is necessary for the democratic nations of the hemisphere to come together and stop this rising threat to peace before it is too late."[10]

Waller proceeds to claim that Chávez runs an "aggressive dictatorship" that "invalidated the existing constitution using illegal and pseudo-legal means and had his supporters write a new constitution."[11] It must be noted here that in 1999, newly elected president Hugo Chávez followed through on one of his initial campaign promises: to draft a new and inclusive constitution with participation by all Venezuelan citizens. That year, in one of the most groundbreaking and pioneering legal processes ever, a constitutional convention was convened with members elected by regional communities throughout the nation. The new constitution was drafted by this convention and then distributed throughout the nation for a period of open commentary. Once all comments, additions, criticisms, and suggestions were received, changes were incorporated and the draft was put to national referendum for a ratification vote. Over 70 percent of voters approved the new constitution and made it law. This constitution, known as the Bolivarian Constitution of 1999, is one of the most expansive documents on human rights known by international law. It even includes a chapter on Indigenous People's rights—not just a clause or an article, but a chapter. Furthermore, the 1999 Bolivarian Constitution guarantees Venezuelans the right "to a dignified life," as well as ensuring the rights to education, health care, housing, work, minimum wage, culture, community media, freedom of information, voting rights, freedom of association, participation in government at all levels, and other rights prescribed under international law.[12]

Clearly, the Center for Security Policy's analysis is not based on fact, but rather is intentionally devised to paint a scary portrait of the Venezuelan government so as to justify its illegal proposals for regime change. In that context, the document goes on to claim that Chávez has "systematically violated the Constitution" and has "stripped the regime's critics of basic human rights and driven hundreds of them into exile."[13] Such statements are sheer fantasy, since Venezuelans enjoy more human rights today than under any prior government. No one has been imprisoned or harassed by the government for their political beliefs. Waller goes further to claim that the August 2004 recall referendum election, during which Chávez's mandate was ratified by 60 percent of voters, equaling almost 6 million votes of the 10 million that voted in that process, was fraudulent. The recall referendum, an electoral option articulated in Article 72 of the Bolivarian Constitution of 1999, was the first of its kind to occur in the world against an elected head of state.

The Organization of American States and the Carter Center, along with more than 170 accredited international observers, all certified the election as legitimate and transparent, and agreed the results were accurate. Even the Department of State reluctantly accepted the outcome.[14]

In the Center for Security Policy paper, these false accusations of how President Chávez has remained in power are coupled with dangerously deceptive allegations about how Chávez threatens the world and therefore why regime change is necessary. Take, for example, the following phony and unsubstantiated claims made by Waller's "What to Do About Venezuela":

Venezuela's Chávez runs an oil-rich dictatorship that has,

- created strategic alliances with designated state-sponsors of terrorism, including Cuba, Iran, Saddam Hussein's Iraq and Libya . . .

- used Venezuela's oil wealth for subversive purposes and to prop up a state sponsor of terrorism . . .

- effectively merged his security and intelligence services with those of Cuba . . .

- aided, abetted, and comforted international Islamist terrorist organizations . . .

- aided and abetted regional narcotics traffickers and narcoterrorists . . .

- aided and abetted narcoguerrilla groups seeking to overthrow the government of Colombia . . .

- developed a coherent, populist political ideology and political action apparatus to spread political subversion in other countries . . .

- is arming to militarize the population and threaten its neighbors . . .

- has curbed civil rights and civil liberties . . .

- is becoming one of the hemisphere's worst violators of human rights . . .

- is trying to limit Washington's latitude for action by cultivating and co-opting decision makers.[15]

It appears as though the last claim is the only accurate one. Venezuela has had relatively limited success in promoting its case in the United States, both within some sectors of Congress and in communities across the nation. Furthermore, Venezuela's regional foreign policy has been extraordinarily successful and prosperous, as neighboring Latin American nations have warmed to its integrationist policies and concepts and have joined with Venezuela to build strong commercial, technological, and social agreements that loosen Washington's grip and domination on the region. Evidently, this success has hurt Washington's giant ego.

All of the other accusations made by Waller and the Center for Security Policy are based on fabricated or inexistent evidence. Again, these are the same claims made in January 2005 by Secretary of State Rice and later regurgitated by ex-Assistant Secretary of State Roger Noriega and CIA Director Porter Goss the following month: Chávez is linked to terrorism, Chávez is a dictator, Chávez is a danger to the region. But more than just rhetoric, the center lays out the "Strategy for Regime Change," a six-part plan that begins by clearly stating, "There is no need for United Nations involvement."[16] Since when does the United States need United Nations involvement or approval to intervene in another country's affairs?

The strategy is also centered on what is referred to as an "information warfare bonanza." "Public education is the key," the document affirms. "The United States must expose the Venezuelan regime and raise awareness of the importance of a new strategy to counter the existing threats."[17] The six general strategy points include:

Helping the dictator hasten his own political demise. The Venezuelan dictator is mentally unstable and has been under psychiatric supervision for years. . . . A psychological profile report in the *New York Times* showed remarkable similarities to that of Saddam Hussein. With lessons learned from the Iraq war, the U.S. can improve its psychological strategy and help the Venezuelan leader to hasten his political self-destruction.

Prevent the dictator from destroying Venezuela's infrastructure . . .

A viable democratic alternative is needed. . . . Friends of democracy throughout the region must provide material support and vocal protection to the remaining opposition members inside the country.

Working with the OAS and Venezuela's internal cycle. . . . First, it can invoke the OAS Democratic Charter. This is the single most powerful weapon against the regime's continued consolidation, and can even be useful in shepherding a reversal of the revolution.

Sustain and protect the democratic and human rights movements inside Venezuela.

Significantly increase cooperation with hemispheric partners to monitor and gather intelligence about the existing partnership between the Venezuelan regime and state sponsors of terrorism, and expose the Bolivarian/terrorist connections.[18]

Finally, the document concludes, "Time is running out. . . . The Bolivarian regime in Caracas presents a clear and present danger to peace and democracy in the hemisphere . . . .U.S. strategy must be to help Venezuela accomplish peaceful change by next year."[19]

Written in May 2005, the next year being referred to is 2006, when presidential elections were looming in December, and it is no coincidence that regime change was being pushed simultaneously by factors in the U.S. government.

The proposed strategies put forth in "What to Do About Venezuela" are precisely the three fronts of action being taken by the U.S. government: financing the opposition movement, taking diplomatic actions against Venezuela (trying to build that "unified international front"), and engaging in military psychological and asymmetric warfare. It is of note that the individuals listed as associated with the Center for Security Policy, either on their board of directors or otherwise related, include individuals from the Bush administration such as Donald Rumsfeld (former secretary of defense), Richard Cheney (vice president), Elliot Abrams (National Security Council), J. D. Crouch (National Security Council), Paula Dobriansky (sub-secretary of state for global affairs), Douglas Feith (ex-sub-secretary of defense policy), Jeane Kirkpatrick (ex-ambassador to the UN), Richard Perle (ex-secretary of joint policy defense at the Pentagon), James Schlesinger (ex-secretary of defense), James Woolsey (ex-CIA director), Henry Hyde (Republican congressman, chairman of the Senate Foreign Relations Committee), Stanley Ebner (lobbyist for Boeing), Charles Kupperman (vice president for space and strategic missiles at Lockheed Martin), Douglas Graham (defense systems director at Lockheed Martin), and Robert Livingston (lobbyist for Raytheon).[20]

Rumsfeld's Concern

Around the same time the Center for Security Policy's strategy report was published, then Secretary of State Donald Rumsfeld made his first public declarations on Venezuela. In a visit to Brazil in late March 2005, Secretary Rumsfeld declared to the press: "Certainly I'm concerned [about the sale of arms to Venezuela]. If one thinks about it, the discussion that's taking place, as I understand it, is concerning something in the neighborhood of 100,000 AK-47s to be moved from Russia possibly to Venezuela. I don't know if it's firm, but I've read about it and heard it discussed. Not just in the press, but bilaterally. I can't imagine what's going to happen to 100,000 AK-47s. I can't imagine why Venezuela needs 100,000 AK-47s. I just hope that, personally hope, that it doesn't happen. I can't imagine that if it did happen, that it would be good for the hemisphere."[21] But when asked later what evidence he actually had that the potential purchase of 100,000 AK-47s from Russia would end up the hands of Colombian guerrillas or other "terrorist," non-military forces, Rumsfeld responded, "I don't have any evidence."[22] Could that be because there is none?

But this admitted lack of evidence did not prevent Rumsfeld or his lower-ranking officials from perpetuating the myth that Chávez was starting a dangerous arms race in the region that was aimed at supplying terrorist and rebel groups with high-level weaponry. Voice of America, the U.S.'s international propaganda outlet, claimed on March 23, 2005, "The United States says it fears the $120 million arms deal could trigger an arms race in the region and lead to the destabilization of Venezuela's neighbors. The United States is especially worried that some of the weapons could end up in the hands of the FARC (the Revolutionary Armed Forces of Colombia), which the United States considers to be a terrorist organization."[23]

In July 2005, a few months later, Rumsfeld's Deputy Assistant Secretary of Defense for Western Hemisphere Affairs, Roger Pardo-Maurer, stated that Venezuela was "evil." Representing the United States government, Pardo-Maurer stood before a group of strategists, analysts, and interested parties at the Hudson Institute's Center for Latin American Studies, and boldly claimed that "there are alternatives to the model that we champion, the model for which we are the champion, which is the model of the demo-cratic, market based liberal society, liberal in the old-fashioned sense of the word . . . . There are less benign alternatives. There are even malicious and I would not be afraid to say, downright evil alternatives. One of them, as we know, is the Bolivarian alternative . . . and this is the model championed by Hugo Chávez in Venezuela."[24]

Deputy Assistant Secretary of Defense Pardo-Maurer goes on to state, "One of the most interesting projects that I've been tracking in Venezuela has to do with the establishment of a militia. Chávez is establishing a militia that will directly report to him, not through any established traditional mil-itary structure. . . . He's purchasing up to 300,000 Kalashnikovs from Russia, and all kinds of other things to support this project."[25] So, now the number is up to 300,000 Kalashnikovs?

Even President George W. Bush hopped on the bandwagon, stating on May 5, 2005, in an interview, "We made our position very clear on the AK-47s to Venezuela, and that is, is that we're concerned that those weapons could end up in the hands of FARC, for example, a very destabilizing force in South America."[26] But remember, Rumsfeld himself admitted publicly that there is "no evidence" to support this position.

In reality, Venezuela's national defense budget in 2005 was $1.61 bil-lion, which places the nation about number 9 on the list of military spend-ing in the hemisphere. The U.S. has a budget more than 400 times larger than Venezuela, with 2005 annual spending in defense exceeding $450 billion. Even Brazil's military budget is 12 times larger than Venezuela's, and other nations, such as Canada, Mexico, Colombia, Chile, Argentina, and possibly Cuba, have substantially higher annual defense budgets than Venezuela.[27] Venezuela did make recent arms acquisitions from Russia and Brazil: planes, helicopters and, yes, Kalashnikov rifles. The rifles used by Venezuela's armed forces were more than forty years old and hadn't been replaced in decades. The majority of the planes and helicopters are for use in counter-narcotics missions and operations. Venezuela, one of the wealthiest oil nations in the world and the richest in this hemisphere, has the sovereign right and duty to ensure its armed forces are well equipped, especially when a world war is being waged for control of ener-gy reserves.

The Aggression Escalates

Throughout the remainder of 2005, the discourse of the Bush administration and its associates grew more aggressive. Stephen Johnson, president of the Heritage Foundation, a Washington-based right-wing think tank, declared Chávez "a dictator that violates human rights, has consolidated power and has maintained his power through electoral fraud in the recall referendum on August 15, 2004."[28] Earlier in the year, in March 2005, the chief of the Southern Command, General Bantz Craddock, declared, "I am concerned about the influence of Venezuela in the area of responsibility. SOUTHCOM supports the position of a joint command to maintain military to military contact with Venezuelan armed forces . . . we need an interagency focus with a wide base to deal with Venezuela." [29] And in late July 2005, Rep. Connie Mack from Florida ranted from the floor of the House of Representatives, "In Hugo Chávez's Venezuela there is no free press just state controlled anti-American propaganda. . . . There is no freedom of speech, no freedom of dissent, and no freedom to stand in opposition to the Chávez regime."[30] Though completely false and ridiculous, considering that the majority of media outlets in Venezuela are privately owned, this statement enabled passage of an amendment to the Foreign Relations Authorization Act that permits broadcasting transmissions into Venezuelan territory to combat President Chávez's "anti-Americanism." The text of the Amendment reads as follows:

> Amendment No. 25 offered by Mr. Mack: Page 24, beginning line 4, add the following new paragraph:
> 5) Broadcasting to Venezuela.—For broadcasting to Venezuela, such sums as may be necessary for fiscal year 2006 and such sums as may be necessary for fiscal year 2007, to remain available until expended, to allow the Broadcasting Board of Governors to carry out broadcasting to Venezuela for at least 30 minutes per day of balanced, objective, and comprehensive television news programming, radio news programming, or both.

Based on this amendment by the House of Representatives, millions of U.S. taxpayer dollars would now be used to broadcast U.S. government propaganda illegally into Venezuela. In early 2007, Congress approved the Senate Foreign Operations Appropriations Bill, adding an additional $10 million for "Broadcasting Voice of America and pro-US messages to Venezuela." Not only is this completely outrageous, but it is unnecessary. In Venezuela, four out of five national broadcast stations are private and controlled by opposition supporters. These channels, along with the vast majority of radio and print media, publish and transmit an anti-Chávez viewpoint during the majority of their airtime every day.[31]

Pat Robertson Wants to "Take Chávez Out"

On August 22, 2005, Reverend Pat Robertson openly and publicly called for the assassination of President Hugo Chávez on his national TV program, *The 700 Club:* "You know, I don't know about this doctrine of assassination, but if he thinks we're trying to assassinate him, I think that we really ought to go ahead and do it. It's a whole lot cheaper than starting a war. And I don't think any oil shipments will stop. But this man is a terrible danger to the United States.... This is in our sphere of influence, so we can't let this happen. We have the Monroe Doctrine, we have other doctrines that we have announced. And without question, this is a dangerous enemy to our south, controlling a huge pool of oil, that could hurt us very badly. We have the ability to take him out, and I think the time has come to exercise that ability. We don't need another $200 billion war to get rid of one, you know, strong-arm dictator. It's a whole lot easier to have some of the covert operatives do the job and then get it over with."[32]

Robertson reaffirmed his comments and his position on President Chávez's assassination on February 3, 2006, this time on the Fox News program *Hannity and Colmes.* When co-host Alan Colmes asked Robertson, "If he [Chávez] were assassinated, the world would be a safer place?" Robertson answered, "I think South America would." When Colmes later pressed Robertson, asking, "Do you want him [Chávez] taken out?" Robertson retorted, "Not now, but one day, one day, one day." Earlier, Colmes had asked, "Should Chávez be assassinated?" Robertson explained that one day Chávez will "be aiming nuclear weapons; and what's coming across the Gulf [of Mexico] isn't going to be [Hurricane] Katrina, it's going to be his nukes." Co-host Sean Hannity agreed that "the world would be better off without him where he [Chávez] is, because he is a danger to the United States."[33] It is no surprise that Fox News agrees with Robertson's view, considering its alliance with the ultra-right wing in the United States.

The Bush administration remained silent with respect to Robertson's comments. Robertson's position, though loopy, bluntly represents the neo-hawks' vision toward Venezuela. Why waste billions on a war or direct intervention when we can just "take him out"? It would not be the first time such a strategy was implemented by Washington in the Latin American region, the area the Monroe Doctrine refers to as "the backyard of the United States." The Monroe Doctrine is not a legal doctrine, but rather a vision laid out by President James Monroe in 1823 which proclaimed that European powers could no longer colonize or intervene in the affairs of the "Americas." The doctrine set forth the hegemonic notion of "America for the Americans," implying U.S. power and domination over the region.[34] It's actually outrageous that Pat Robertson so lightly invokes the Monroe Doctrine as a legitimate instrument of international foreign policy that would enable the United States to execute a leader it considers "threatens" its interests.

Shift from Diplomacy to the War Machine

The year 2006 began with another major shift in U.S. policy toward Venezuela. Even though throughout 2005 voices from the Defense Department and the CIA had made harsh statements about Venezuela, it had yet to become a major priority for these entities. But all that changed in 2006. John Negroponte, Director of National Intelligence, indicated this shift in his opening comments before the Senate Select Committee on Intelligence on February 2, 2006: "In Venezuela, President Chávez, if he wins reelection later this year, appears ready to use his control of the legislature and other institutions to continue to stifle the opposition, reduce press freedom, and entrench himself through measures that are technically legal, but which nonetheless constrict democracy. We expect Chávez to deepen his relationship with Castro. Venezuela provides roughly two-thirds of that island's oil needs on preferential credit terms. He also is seeking closer economic, military, and diplomatic ties with Iran and North Korea. Chávez has scaled back counter-narcotics cooperation with the U.S. Increased oil revenues have allowed Chávez to embark on an activist foreign policy in Latin America that includes providing oil at favorable repayment rates to gain allies, using newly created media outlets to generate support for his Bolivarian goals, and meddling in the internal affairs of his neighbors by backing particular candidates for elective office."[35]

On that very same day, almost as though it had been coordinated, in an appearance before the National Press Club, Secretary of State Donald Rumsfeld compared Chávez to Adolf Hitler: "We've got Chávez in Venezuela with a lot of oil money. He's a person who was elected legally, just as Adolf Hitler was elected legally, and then consolidated power, and now is of course working closely with Fidel Castro and Mr. Morales [Bolivian president Evo Morales] and others. It concerns me."[36]

So now Negroponte, head of the U.S. intelligence community, and Rumsfeld, in charge of the Pentagon, are both referring to Chávez as a dictator who relates to terrorist states (Iran and North Korea), fails to collaborate on counter-narcotics operations, and intervenes in the affairs of neighboring nations in an allegedly destabilizing fashion. Intelligence and Defense: these are the two entities that make war. Referring to Chávez as a "Hitler" is a very serious charge. World War II was convened to take out Hilter. And the relation made between Chávez and Iran and North Korea is also alarming, since both are considered dangerous enemy nations by the United States government, which is flirting with the idea of a possible invasion or attack. Therefore, the reference and comparison to Chávez is a matter of great concern.

On March 16, 2006, George W. Bush announced a revision of his National Security Strategy, which had been released originally in 2002. For the first time in history, Venezuela was referred to in the text as a dangerous threat to U.S. security interests. In Section IV (B), "Successes and Challenges," the document states, "In Venezuela, a demagogue awash in oil money is undermining democracy and seeking to destabilize the region."[37] The inclusion of Venezuela in a National Security Strategy that ratified the concept of "preemptory, unilateral war" when the U.S. believes a threat to its interests exists, is very revealing regarding present U.S. policy toward the South American nation. During just a one-year period, Venezuela transformed from what Condoleezza Rice termed a "negative force" to become a "threat to National Security."

Just what makes Venezuela such a serious threat to U.S. interests? Besides the fact that it supplies 15 percent of oil consumed in the United States, is one of the closest suppliers (it only takes between 4 to 6 days to ship Venezuelan oil to the U.S., whereas it can take up to 6–8 weeks to transport oil from the Middle East to U.S. soil), and has 14,000 gas stations and 7 refineries inside the United States, Venezuela represents a challenge to Washington's model of neoliberal capitalist democracy that has been presented to the world as "the best model of democracy." Venezuela's revolutionary democracy, or Bolivarian socialism of the twenty-first century, seriously poses an ideological and economic alternative to the failing U.S. model. President Bush made it very clear that the hemisphere would have to choose between these two models in order to move forward in peace. In remarks made in Brazil after the Summit of the Americas meeting in November 2005 in Mar de Plata, Argentina, where Bush's Free Trade of the Americas Agreement was shot down by a majority of South American nations, he declared, "Ensuring social justice in the Americas requires choosing between two rival visions. One offers hope and is based on representative democracy, integration into the world community and faith in the transforming power of liberty in individuals' lives. The other seeks to reverse democratic achievements during the last two decades, appealing to fear, confrontation between neighbors and blaming others for its own failures in not bringing prosperity to its people."[38] Clearly, Venezuela's model was now viewed as an equal rival to the United States, an incredible achievement for a developing South American nation in just a little more than five years.

Terrorism

When the State Department's annual report on terrorism was released in spring 2006, Venezuela was labeled as "negligible" in its cooperation.

"Venezuelan cooperation in the international campaign against terrorism remained negligible. President Hugo Chávez persisted in public criticism of U.S. counterterrorism efforts, publicly championed Iraqi terrorists, deepened Venezuelan collaboration with such state sponsors of terrorism as Cuba and Iran. . . .It is unclear whether and to what extent the government of Venezuela provided material support to Colombian terrorists, and at what level."[39] Thomas Shannon, then Assistant Secretary of State for Western Hemisphere Affairs, subsequently made several severe statements about Venezuela, indicating a harshening of policy toward the nation. "Cuban intelligence has effectively cloned itself inside Venezuelan intelligence," Shannon told editors and reporters at the *Washington Times*. He also claimed that "Venezuela is providing shelter for organizations with ties to unspecified terrorist organizations in the Middle East," indicating that Hezbollah was one of the organizations.[40] Sounds like information based on the document authored by former ambassador Charles Shapiro, who alleged that Hezbollah and related groups were operating out of Venezuelan territory, though no evidence has ever been offered to prove such allegations.

In an unprecedented move, Shannon confirmed to the *Washington Times* reporters that Venezuela would be "designated a country that is not fully cooperating with efforts against terrorism," which makes it the only country with that designation that is not also on the list of state sponsors of terrorism. The designation, an invention of the U.S. government by its own rules, allows Washington to unilaterally ban Venezuela from purchasing U.S. weapons or weapons made with U.S. parts. Venezuela is the first nation in the world to receive such a designation without also being labeled a "state sponsor of terrorism," inching it further toward inclusion on the list of terrorist countries. Venezuela has never physically threatened U.S. interests, citizens, or ever attacked or threatened to attack the United States or its interests.

Two months later, in July 2006, the Subcommittee on International Terrorism and Nonproliferation of the House of Representatives hosted a hearing titled "Venezuela: Terrorism Hub of South America?" Chairman of the subcommittee Rep. Ed Royce declared in his opening statement at the hearing that "Venezuela, under President Hugo Chávez, has tolerated terrorists on its soil and has forged close relations with officially designated state sponsors of terrorism: Cuba, Iran and North Korea. Colombian terrorist groups use Venezuelan territory for safe haven. . . . There are other worrisome reports of radical Islamist activity in Venezuela. State Department officials have expressed concerns about 'groups and individuals' in Venezuela with 'links to terrorist organizations in the Middle East.' The al-Qaeda, Hamas and Hezbollah cells in South and Central America are tied to fund-raising and transnational criminal networks that are key to terrorist mobility. Three years ago, an intelligence official was quoted as saying with respect to terrorism in Latin America, 'We don't even know what we don't know.' I can't be sure that this has changed."

Is this what U.S. foreign policy on terrorism in Latin America is based on? "We don't even know what we don't know" so let's just take 'em all out? Or classify nations as terrorist or almost-terrorist based on bogus and inflated news and intelligence reports? It is frightening to think that Venezuela has been placed on a list that the U.S government can use to justify preemptive war based on "what we don't know." None of the claims that Venezuela harbors terrorist groups have ever been substantiated. In fact, they all seem to originate from the 2003 *U.S. News and World Report* article that Chairman Ed Royce refers to in his statement before the committee (it's the only "evidence" cited by Royce in his declaration).

Journalist Linda Robinson authored a fantastical piece based on fable and fiction in October 2003 and got it front and center. "Terror Close to Home" was the headline, and the entire article was filled with made-up data about terrorist training camps in Venezuela. The article was later disproved and refuted by the then chief of the Southern Command, James Hill, who confirmed that "no such evidence existed."[41] This is a true example of how misinformation works. Despite the absolute disclaiming of the veracity of Robinson's article, it has been recycled and cited by high level officials in the U.S. government and other news entities. This is how lies become truths that are used to justify war.

In just one year's time, Venezuela was virtually labeled as a "terrorist nation" by Washington, and Bush himself constantly confessed to the press that he's "worried about Venezuela," and "that Chávez is really hurtin' the country."[42] And sure enough, in March 2007, the State Department released again its annual report on terrorism, labeling Venezuela as "not fully cooperating" with U.S. counterterrorism efforts.[43] The report ratified the sanction against Venezuela, prohibiting the sale of arms to the South American nation from the United States or from nations or companies that use U.S. technology in the manufacture of their weapons. Considering that Venezuela traditionally has maintained its commercial relationship with the United States, a majority of its arms had always been acquired from the U.S. or related companies. Therefore, this prohibition—two years in a row— caused Venezuela to reorient its weapons purchases, looking to other countries with little U.S. ties for its arms supply, such as Russia, China, and Iran. Even neighboring nations like Brazil were forced to break contracts with Venezuela for the sale of surveillance airplanes (Super Toucans), which would have aided Venezuela's counter-narcotics efforts. Both Spain and Norway were also forced by the United States to break contracts for sales of military aircraft and technologies to Venezuela.

One of the U.S. criticisms of the Venezuelan government has been its increased ties to nations such as Russia, China, and Iran, indicating that some type of threatening axis is being formed among these nations against the United States. However, U.S. sanctions and prohibitions have been the major cause of these relationships, as Venezuela, desiring to develop its infrastructure and economy, has been forced to seek out technology and resources from nations other than the U.S. As the U.S. global war on terrorism expands throughout the Middle East and threatens Iran, Cuba, and other nations, it becomes clear that Venezuela is one of the newest targets of U.S. aggression. In two years, Venezuela has quickly moved to become a major target and priority for the U.S and is now considered one of the most threatening nations in the world to U.S. interests.

3

The Money Pot Grows:
The National Endowment for Democracy

In February 2006, President George W. Bush made a request to Congress for an extraordinarily high amount of funding of "democracy initiatives" in Latin America. Of this elevated budget proposal, $143.7 million was slated for "promoting the objectives" of his administration in Latin America and the Caribbean, particularly those associated with collective security and strengthening institutions and democratic practices. An additional $26.8 million of funding was to be directed toward the "consolidation of democratic advances" in Bolivia, Brazil, Ecuador, Paraguay, Perú and Venezuela. Separately, Bush indicated that in the case of Venezuela, the funds would be destined for "supporting the efforts of political party formation and non-governmental organizations' programs focused on the development of democracy."[1]

Sound innocent?

The National Endowment for Democracy's role in funding the groups and parties that executed the April 2002 coup against President Chávez is amply documented, proven beyond a reasonable doubt.[2] NED's so-called mission to promote democracy abroad has been significantly perverted in the case of Venezuela, though other investigators have discovered similar cases in Haiti, Nicaragua, Ukraine, Belarus, Russia, and even Ethiopia. The government of Ethiopia expelled three U.S. organizations funded by NED and the United States Agency for International Development in March 2005, alleging that representatives from the International Republican

Institute (IRI), the National Democratic Institute (NDI), and the International Foundation for Electoral Systems (IFES) had illegally entered the country and set up offices without visas or other authorization from the Ethiopian government.[3]

Such practices are not unusual for these organizations, since they are endowed with the U.S. imperialist belief that the world is their hunting ground and the United States can set up operations in any weaker nation without permission. The same pattern was repeated in Venezuela when NED and USAID first arrived prominently on the scene back in 2001. Permission was never requested from the Venezuelan government, despite the undeniable fact that NED and USAID are funded and supervised by the Department of State and Congress, which makes them U.S. government organizations. U.S. funding of foreign governments is not permitted by law and even those non-governmental organizations that receive government funding must be "registered" as "foreign agents" with the Department of Justice under the Foreign Agent Registration Act (FARA) and must report frequently to the Department of Justice on all activities conducted with foreign government funding and direction in detail. [4]

The Russian government has accused the International Republican Institute (IRI) and other NED- and USAID-funded organizations operating in Russia and other Eastern European countries of engaging in acts of espionage and conspiring to induce another "colored revolution" in neighboring Belarus. "U.S., British and other foreign non-governmental organizations are providing cover for professional spies in Russia, while Western organizations are bankrolling plans to stage peaceful revolutions in Belarus and other former Soviet republics bordering Russia," declared Federal Security Service director Nikolai Patrushev back in May 2005.[5]

And in Haiti, NED and USAID have been accused of bankrolling the 2004 coup d'état against President Jean Bertrand Aristide and engaging in propaganda techniques by financing Associated Press reporters who have filtered stories into U.S. media, such as the *New York Times*, in efforts to paint a legitimate and favorable image of their work in that nation. "A by-lined freelancer for the Associated Press, who is also a stringer for the *New York Times* in Haiti, is moonlighting as a consultant for the US government funded National Endowment for Democracy, according to an official at

NED, and several of the agency's grantees . . . . Regine Alexandre, whose name appears as an AP by-line at least a dozen times starting in May of 2004, and appears as a contributor to two *New York Times* stories, is a part of a NED 'experiment' to place a representative on the ground in countries where NED has funded groups. 'This is almost like an experiment for us,' said Fabiola Cordova, a Haiti program officer with NED in Washington on December 6th."[6] When the U.S. government covertly funds journalists to write stories that favorably portray its policies and agenda, the result is propaganda.

NED funding in Haiti skyrocketed from zero dollars in 2003 to more than half a million dollars in fiscal 2005, during and following the period that President Aristide was illegally removed from power. At the same time, the International Republican Institute, created back in 1983 as one of the four core groups of NED, overseen by the Republican Party and currently chaired by Senator John McCain, began funding and training more than 600 anti-Aristide activists and leaders in 2002 and 2003.[7] In 2004, many of those same individuals were fundamental in the street riots and protests that eventually resulted in the overthrow of Haiti's democratically elected president.[8] The strategy that had failed in Venezuela subsequently succeeded in Haiti.

Since 2005, NED and USAID funding in Venezuela has remained substantial. The total sum invested in the years 2000–4 in opposition groups in Venezuela was approximately $27 million in U.S. taxpayer dollars. For the years 2005–7, NED was granted more than $3 million for its Venezuela activities and USAID issued approximately $7.2 million for its Caracas-based Office of Transition Initiatives and other Venezuela programs.[9] USAID still refuses to include specific sections for Venezuela on its website, since clearly its work in that nation has been revealed as a sham and a cover for illegal activity, but its budget request for its Venezuela operations is available.[10]

Where was this money going? In the case of the National Endowment for Democracy, the fiscal 2005 groups receiving the funding are as follows:

Mexico and Venezuela
American University
$171,538: To promote the role of legal academia in influencing public policy in human rights. In Mexico, AU will work with its partner institutions to produce a research report and model draft legislation to amend

the current legislation on the prohibition of torture. In Venezuela, AU will help five universities develop teaching capacity and a curriculum in the area of human rights protection and promotion.

Andean Region
American Center for International Labor Solidarity
$637,327: To strengthen unions' capacity to involve workers in the practice of democracy at their workplaces and in broader economic and political arenas. Economic and technical support will be provided for strategic development of contract proposals, negotiations, and support actions for unions. A series of two-day workshops for negotiators and union leadership to develop specific negotiation proposals and plans for advancing and negotiating the proposals will be held in Bolivia, Colombia, Ecuador, Peru and Venezuela.

The Center for Justice and International Law (CEJIL)
$140,000: To promote and defend human rights in Colombia, Ecuador, Peru, and Venezuela. CEJIL will continue to present and litigate cases before the Inter-American System (IAS), train human rights activists, journalists, and young leaders in international human rights standards and the use of the IAS, and support and encourage local NGOs and civil society organizations in their efforts to defend human rights.

Center for International Private Enterprise (CIPE)-CEDICE
$148,750: To promote good corporate governance in Colombia, Ecuador, and Venezuela. CIPE will work with the Colombian Confederation of Chambers of Commerce, local participating organizations of the Quito Stock Exchange, and the Association of Venezuelan Executives to build a network of private sector institutions to strengthen the culture of good governance and improve democratic dialogue with government policy makers.

Latin America Regional
Afro-América XXI Colombia Chapter
$90,530: To promote local political participation of Afro-Latino organ-

izations and leaders in Honduras, Peru, and Venezuela. XXI Colombia will train 75 community leaders from 30 Afro-Latino grassroots organizations in institutional strengthening, leadership and civil and political rights. XXI Colombia will also establish working groups with local government officials in the three countries.

Canadian Foundation for the Americas
$94,516: To generate a dialogue on the role that civil society and the international community can play in the promotion and defense of democracy in the hemisphere. FOCAL will commission two papers, organize a Conference in Ottawa, and conduct follow-up meetings in Venezuela and Ecuador on civil society and hemispheric and international norms for democracy promotion and defense.

Instituto de Prensa y Sociedad (Institute for Press and Society)
$105,770: To protect journalists in Peru, expand its access to information and civic journalism initiatives domestically, and continue promoting an Andean network to protect journalists in Colombia and Venezuela. The network enables a journalist who is in trouble or the victim of an attack to report the threat or attack to the central office in Lima, after which IPYS will investigate and publicize the attack, and provide legal assistance to the journalist, if necessary.

Venezuela
International Republican Institute
$200,000: To promote more responsive political parties. IRI will assist political parties in improving their capacity to identify and represent constituent concerns; adopting clear and concise party platforms and communicating them to voters; and developing internal structures and processes for transparent and democratic selection of party leaders.

Asociación Civil Consorcio Desarrollo y Justicia (Development and Justice Consortium)
$74,590: To promote more efficient and independent judicial systems. The consortium will continue its Andean regional judicial observatory,

monitoring key aspects of the judicial systems in Venezuela, Peru, and Ecuador with the assistance of human rights organizations in those countries. The Consortium will also continue its collaboration with the Peruvian NGO Instituto de Defensa Legal (Legal Defense Institute) to conduct a democracy leadership training program for community and Afro-Venezuelan and indigenous leaders in Venezuela.

Instituto Prensa y Sociedad—Venezuela (Press and Society Institute—Venezuela)
$74,950: To promote freedom of expression and journalist profession-alization and safety. IPYS-Venezuela will maintain its alert network through continued support to correspondents in seven provinces to monitor press conditions and investigate cases of attacks or threats against journalists. IPYS-Venezuela will also offer training workshops for journalists' professionalization on such topics as investigative report-ing, journalist ethics, and the role of the media in promoting demo-cratic values.

Asociación Civil Uniandes
$15,058: To promote local participation in social welfare programs in Mérida. Uniandes will train 30 community organizations in public advo-cacy, help organize them into a state-wide network, and work with local governments to improve links between these organizations and local authorities.

Centro al Servicio de la Acción Popular (Center at the Service of Popular Action)
$68,133: To promote community participation in the planning and implementation of social programs. CESAP will work with local groups in Zulia, Anzoátegui, and Trujillo states to monitor government budgets and programs, gather data through surveys, and train local organizations on how to participate in the planning, implementation, and evaluation of social programs in Venezuela. CESAP will also continue to produce a regular report on poverty and social programs at the local level in Venezuela.

Acción Campesina (Farmers in Action)

$58,240: To promote farmers' rights at national and local levels through policy reform at the local level. Acción Campesina will work with local organizations in four states to analyze local conditions, develop proposals for policy and legislation concerning agriculture and rural development, and promote those initiatives to local, state, and national public officials.

Asociación Civil Consorcio Justicia-Occidente (Civil Association "Justice Consortium"—West)

$20,000: To strengthen community leadership and peaceful resolution of conflict. Consorcio Justicia-Occidente will work with local community organizations in the state of Táchira, on the border of Colombia, to train over 400 young community leaders in democratic leadership, democratic values and human rights. Consorcio Justicia-Occidente will then work with these leaders in their communities to help them carry out projects to develop strategies for addressing local problems.

Asociación Civil Justicia Alternativa (Civil Association "Justice Consortium")

$17,650: To promote the political participation of youth and the peaceful resolution of conflict. Working with local middle and high schools, Justicia Alternativa will convene five workshops that will teach students the tools and meaning of democratic leadership. Justicia Alternativa will also conduct four workshops to bring together community representatives and locally elected officials to discuss ways of improving collaboration between communities and local officials.

Asociación Civil Kapé-kapé (Civil Association "Kapé-kapé")

$14,950: To strengthen civil society among indigenous communities of Bolívar and Delta Amacuro states. Kapé-kapé will conduct 20 leadership and conflict resolution workshops in the Warao and Pemón communities. Drawing from the communities' traditional means of conflict resolution and other methods of negotiation, the participants in the workshop will develop an agenda for addressing economic, social, and political problems confronting the Warao and Pemón communities.

Asociación Civil Liderazgo y Visión (Civil Association "Leadership and Vision")

$22,721: To conduct a democracy and human rights training program for public servants in Carabobo state. Liderazgo y Visión will train a total of 550 police officers and firemen in democratic rights and responsibilities and the peaceful resolution of conflict. In addition, Liderazgo y Visión will train a total of twelve representatives to serve as coordinators for follow-up and to help organize and conduct courses and informal workshops in the future.

Centro por la Resolución de Conflictos de la Asociación de Abogados del Estado Lara (Center for the Resolution of Conflict of the Lawyers Association of the state of Lara)

$12,850: To promote tolerance and nonviolence in Lara State. The Center will conduct workshops on conflict resolution and dialogue and organize eight dialogue tables in the city of Barquisimeto. The dialogue tables will bring together four representatives that support the national governing party and four representatives from groups that oppose the national governing party to jointly develop action plans for commonly identified community problems.

Concentroccidente

$14,202: To promote the political representation of informal sector business owners and employees in Lara State in western Venezuela. Concentroccidente will convene three workshops that will bring together informal and micro-enterprise representatives and associations from different sectors of the economy, including manufacturing, sales, and services, to establish a network to advocate their interests at the local and national level.

Fundación Justicia de Paz del Estado Monagas (Justice of Peace of Monagas State Foundation)

$17,200: To train police and communities in human rights. Fundación Justicia de Paz will conduct 10 workshops on constitutionally protected human rights and tools for improving relationships with local communi-

ties for over 300 police officers in the state of Monagas. To complement
its work within the police forces, Fundación Justicia de Paz will hold 12
community forums throughout the city of Maturín to discuss concerns
and issues with the local police.

Súmate
$107,200: To educate citizens on the election law and to encourage and
provide them with the tools to claim their right to free, open, and transparent elections. Súmate will conduct 360 training workshops in all 24 states,
training a total of 12,200 members of its national network of volunteers in
elections law. The workshops will train volunteers and local citizens in the
"five requisites for a clean election," which have been cited consistently by
Venezuelans and international election observation groups.

Venezolanos del Mundo (Venezuelans of the World)
$12,490: To improve and professionalize community journalism. The
project will conduct 50 workshops with networks of community journalists to improve their ability to cover local events objectively and respon-
sibly and share with them methods of investigative journalism.
Venezolanos del Mundo will also hold five community workshops in
poorer neighborhoods in and around Caracas to bring together residents
and journalists to discuss local issues and ways in which they can collaborate to promote common objectives.[11]

Many of these Venezuelan organizations are the same groups that have
been receiving NED monies throughout the past few years, such as Súmate,
Liderazgo y Visión, Consorcio Justicia, CESAP, CEDICE, Acción
Campesina, and Justicia Alternativa, along with U.S. institutions working
with the same opposition groups in-country, including CEJIL, CIPE, and
the IPYS (Press and Society Institute). However, there is an alarming
change in NED Venezuela-based financing: it appears as though NED has
reached into communities that generally support the Venezuelan government and particularly President Chávez in an attempt to buy them, or "win
their hearts and minds." Note specifically the direction of funding to indigenous groups (Asociación Civil Kapé Kapé) and Afro-Venezuelan communi-

ties (Consorcio Justicia and Afro-America XXI). There are also indications that NED is seeking to expand its influence into the growing community media movement in Venezuela by funding the creation of the group Venezolanos del Mundo (Venezuelans of the World) to penetrate and "train" community media activists and journalists. Venezuela's only true free and independent media is its community media, since private media are all owned by a wealthy Venezuelan elite that has been engaging in an intense media war in support of efforts to remove Chávez from power.

What is wrong with receiving financing from the U.S. government through NED? Is all the work these groups are doing bad? Many have asked these questions.

Some of the groups are outspoken anti-Chávez organizations, like Liderazgo y Visión, which continues to state in its project reports comments such as, "Venezuela, a nation that once had the most stable democracy in South America, now suffers a severe crisis of governance."[12] Or others, such as Súmate, which has been unfettered in its attempts to discredit Venezuela's electoral system and has tried to portray its members as "victims" of political persecution, is a renowned opposition group. (More on this organization will be discussed in the following chapter.) And there are groups such as CEDICE that publish articles and information from opposition leaders ranting and raving about the evils of the Chávez government and whose director, Rocio Guijarro, was a key signatory of the Carmona Decree that abolished all of Venezuela's democratic institutions. In fact, members of Liderazgo y Visión and Súmate were also signers of the Carmona Decree, proving their very undemocratic credentials.[13]

But other groups, such as Consorcio Justicia or CESAP, for example, may occasionally pursue decent projects that have minor benefits on a local level, depending on the success of their initiatives.

At the same time, NED monies are not unconditional. The groups are supervised by NED and U.S. embassy officials and held on a very tight leash. NED can influence the types of materials used in projects and how programs are implemented, including their underlying ideology, and therein lies the major problem regarding this funding.

Carl Gershman, president of NED since 1984, is unquestionably anti-Chávez. The latest NED literature classifies Venezuela as a "semi-authoritarian" country, where "democratic progress has been stalled or been reversed." These are very deceptive claims. A majority of Venezuelan citizens believe that the Chávez government is the most democratic and participatory government the nation has ever had. More Venezuelans are included and engaged in the political and economic sphere than at any time before in history, and the millions of Venezuelans who in prior decades were marginalized and isolated from government are now active participants in the construction of a new, more democratic society. Cooperatives and community-based councils and organizations are promoted by the government so that every citizen has the opportunity to access and influence politics and governance for the benefit of all. Thousands of new voting centers have been placed throughout the nation, even in the poorest "barrios," so that every eligible voter has access to the electoral process. Voting drives consistently ensure that all eligible voters are registered so they can exercise the sacred right to vote. This is a true democracy.

But Carl Gershman believes otherwise. Or, at least he tries to convince us that he believes otherwise. Gershman has created the terms "hybrid regimes" and "semi-authoritarian democracies" to refer to Venezuela and other nations that have publicly questioned the intentions of NED funding in their countries. Who are the lucky ones to receive this classification? Ethiopia, Russia, and Venezuela, the very nations that have made public the illegal and undermining activities of NED that promote attempts to overthrow their governments.

Gershman, in "New Threats to Freedom" in the *Journal of Democracy*,[14] claims: "Hybrid regimes often retain certain formally democratic procedures, including relatively free (if not fair) elections, and permit civil society organizations to function and receive foreign assistance. But the underlying political realities are manipulated elections, a weak parliament, an overweening executive branch, state-controlled media, rampant corruption, and no recourse to an independent judiciary."[15] Actually, that sort of "hybrid regime" sounds like the reality of the United States under George W. Bush.

Gershman further amplifies the meaning of "hybrid regimes" by stating they are "illiberal, backsliding, or fraudulent democracies or partially open dictatorships."[16] In the case of Venezuela, Gershman takes it a step further and classifies President Chávez's government as a "backsliding autocracy" that was "once an electoral democracy but . . . democratic rights and processes have been steadily eroded and international assistance to democratic NGOs have increasingly come under attack."[17] That statement reveals the true motivation behind Gershman's senseless and angry lashing out at Venezuela: his institution has been exposed for subverting and undermining democracy instead of promoting it, and the undemocratic actions of his pet groups, such as Súmate, have also been uncovered. As a result of this exposure and the Venezuelan and other governments' actions to prevent NED from conspiring against their democratically elected administrations, Gershman's more than twenty years of work as the head of NED has come under serious scrutiny.

Gershman has been left hanging by one arm, gripping at every shred of power and authority that remains within his grasp and has appealed to the international community to legitimize his institution's subversive tactics as an "international norm." He has attempted to shield and amplify his work through the creation of the World Movement for Democracy, an allegedly "global network of democrats who have come together to cooperate in the promotion of democracy" and whose secretariat is none other than the National Endowment for Democracy.[18]

My Encounter with Carl Gershman

In 2005 I had the opportunity to attend an annual meeting of the World Movement for Democracy in Stockholm, Sweden. I was invited to speak on a panel at the "World Meeting of Democracy-Promoting Foundations" by one of seven political parties represented in the Swedish Parliament. The meeting was held in the main chamber of Parliament, August 28–30, 2005, and I had been slated to speak on a panel "Supporting Regime Change—Democratic Assistance or Intervention?" alongside none other than Carl Gershman, president of the National Endowment for Democracy. After confirming that I would attend, my air ticket purchased by the conference organizers, I was informed approximately one week before the event that, for technical reasons, I had been removed from the panel as a speaker but would still be invited to attend the meeting as a participant. Members of the Leftist Party from Sweden had informed me that the true motive behind my removal was Carl Gershman's statement that he "refused to be on a panel with me" and that it was either "him or me." Obviously, considering NED is the secretariat of the organization, the decision was made to keep him and not me. But I went to Stockholm that August 28 with a clear conscience and an open mind, interested to see how the meeting would be conducted.

The night before the first day of panel sessions there was a reception at the residence of the county governor of Stockholm, Mr. Mats Hellström. I attended the reception along with Eva Björkland, the member of the Leftist Party who had arranged for my invitation. As we mingled among "world democracy promoters" drinking wine and eating smoked salmon and cheese in the governor's garden, I was introduced to Walden Bello, executive director of Focus on the Global South in the Philippines, who would be one of the opening speakers the following day. We informed Walden of the events leading to my removal from the panel and the true motivation behind such an act, and Walden decided to make a formal plea to the "promoters of democracy" that my voice be heard. At the end of his speech the next morning, Walden Bello followed through on his promise of the night before and asked the organizers and the participants to reinstate my participation on the "regime change" panel, adding that it seemed inappropriate for leaders of organizations that allegedly support and promote democracy to exclude voices of criticism. Walden's calls were echoed by many in the audience, yet the organizers remained firm in their decision to keep me off the panel.

That afternoon, after the lunch break where participants were abuzz with intrigue about the removal of "the Venezuelan" from the "regime change" panel, I patiently sat through Carl Gershman's offensive remarks about President Chávez being a "semi-dictator" and running a "hybrid, semi-authoritarian regime," and noted his angry and aggressive tone. I listened with full attention to Abir Alsahlani of the Iraqi Democratic Alliance, an NED-funded group, explain to the audience how the occupation in Iraq was a necessary step toward democracy. And I even withstood Maria Leissner, former leader of Sweden's right-wing Liberal Party, as she explained how the only acceptable form of democracy is a representative democracy, and all others were considered dictatorships or hybrids thereof. Leissner's tone was direct and straightforward, especially about the work of democracy-promoting organizations: "Let's call what we do for what it is: intervention. And we will keep doing it until all nations become representative democracies."

When the time came for questions and answers, I dutifully raised my hand and waited to be called on. Others in the audience criticized and questioned Gershman's vicious and tainted remarks about Venezuela, and again called for my reinstatement to the panel. At last I was given the turn to speak, "though brief," I was told, and I calmly and respectfully addressed Mr. Gershman and said how I believed the National Endowment for Democracy had a noble mission and objective to promote democracy around the world, yet sometimes, as in the case of Venezuela, that mission hasn't been completed and, instead of promoting democracy, NED has actually subverted and undermined the democratic process. I expressed my belief that NED and other democracy-promoting foundations should allow for criticism, and more importantly, be self-critical, so as to ensure that their delicate and noble mission is truly being accomplished by the best means possible. I closed by simply stating that I hadn't been informed of the true reasons behind my removal from the panel, but had I been on it, I basically would have just said the same thing.

Well, let me tell you, dear reader, what was to follow was most unexpected by everyone in the Swedish Parliament that day. Carl Gershman looked at me as though I was the incarnation of all evil. He became red in the face and began pounding his fists on the podium. "Do you want to know why you were removed from this panel?" he snarled. "I'll tell you why. I removed you. I refused to be on a panel with someone like you. You disgust me." In a voice of sheer rage, Mr. Carl Gershman, president of the noble National Endowment for Democracy that "promotes democracy" in more than seventy countries around the world, asked, "Do you think we need two points of view on this panel for every issue? I don't think so. If I had wanted a jurist on this panel from Venezuela it would have been a distinguished one, like Carlos Ayala, instead of one like you who supports a criminal regime." Yes, the man in charge of an $80 billion budget to engage in democracy initiatives around the world had just shown his true authoritarian spirit. Two points of view? For what purpose? It was only his that counted, only his that was valid. And in the distinguished Swedish Parliament with beautifully decorated ceilings, Carl Gershman had shown us on that August afternoon what NED's version of democracy was all about.

Swedish papers headlined the following day, "NED Silences Critical Voice," detailing the developments of the Gershman-Golinger incident and questioning how the National Endowment for Democracy can purport to promote democracy when its own president is autocratic. In the end, the event was a success for us true believers in democratic principles.

USAID's Secrets

USAID's funding programs in Venezuela have become more secretive since the release of *The Chávez Code*. USAID has denied the release of the names of the groups it funds in Venezuela based on an abuse of FOIA Exemption (b)(6), which protects individuals from an "unwarranted invasion of privacy."[19] But organizations and entities have no privacy rights under the law, and such an application of Exemption (b)(6) is clearly illegal. At present, this issue is being pursued in the Federal District Court in Washington, D.C., and the results may still not be known by the time this book is published.

In any case, the mere fact that USAID would invoke this exemption clearly indicates their desire to cover up the agency's activities in Venezuela. USAID has never clarified why the Office of Transition Initiatives in Caracas has been extended indefinitely, despite initial claims that it would only remain in Venezuela for two years.[20] The 2006 and 2007 budget indicates that the OTI has been allocated $3.6 million per year for its work in Venezuela, yet USAID refuses to reveal precisely how those funds are being spent. This is a clear abuse of U.S. taxpayer dollars, since citizens have the right to know how their money is being distributed, particularly in the case of public funds sent for democracy initiatives in a foreign nation. Furthermore, USAID is technically not a secret agency, nor is its work officially classified as "national security." However, the position USAID has assumed with respect to its funding projects in Venezuela clearly causes us to question the motivations and intentions behind such work.

Ambassador William Brownfield, the State Department's representative in Venezuela from 2004 to2007, became the public champion of USAID's funding in Venezuela. It became his diplomatic ballgame, filled with lots of provocations, fouls and outs, and occasionally a base hit. His interventionist actions are explored in chapter 10.

What is clear from the increase in NED funding in Venezuela and USAID's ongoing OTI program and multimillion-dollar budget is that the money is still flowing from the U.S. government into the pockets of Venezuela's opposition sector.

4

Súmate in Bush's Hands

Maria Corina Machado, director of Súmate with
President George W. Bush, May 31, 2005, Associated Press

On May 31, 2005, Maria Corina Machado, director of the Venezuelan
organization Súmate, was the first Venezuelan to be officially received in the
Oval Office by President George W. Bush. In fact, she was the first
Venezuelan to be publicly received in Bush's White House, period. No
member of the Chávez administration has ever been invited to meet with a
U.S. official in Washington, let alone the president. Machado met for more
than fifty minutes with President Bush, alone. At the end of the meeting, the

press was invited in for a photo-op and the all-telling image was captured of Machado and Bush, hand in hand. Following the meeting, Machado was given the opportunity to hold a press conference on the White House lawn, a space generally reserved for the president and other heads of state. Machado told reporters that she "was invited by President Bush because he's very interested to know the perspective of civil society about democratic values and the spread of democracy, in particular, in my country, Venezuela."[1] She also said, "We discussed these visions, and I gave him the reassurance that we Venezuelans want to live in democracy and freedom and that we're working hard for it and that we realize this is our job: to maintain and defend democracy in Venezuela."[2]

Sounds sweet, but is it?

It is rare for the president of the United States to meet for such long periods (50 minutes is an eternity for Bush) with a member of a non-governmental organization from an officially friendly foreign nation. The meeting with Machado, the public face of Súmate, was calculated to send a clear statement to the Chávez government that Washington views Súmate as its actor in Venezuela and will do whatever it takes to protect the group. Machado, a signer of the April 2002 Carmona Decree, which authorized the installation of a dictatorship, portrays herself as a soft, fragile yet strong human rights and democracy activist. In her press conference on the White House lawn, Machado again denied she had signed the "decree," but her signature is on the document, and it matches her signature on all NED grants for her organization.

In September 2003, Súmate was given a $53,000 grant from the National Endowment for Democracy, supposedly to promote "election education."[3] These funds were immediately invested in the efforts to hold a recall referendum against President Chávez. Despite NED's claim that it does not "fund groups based upon their support for or opposition to the government" and that "all of the programs we fund operate on a nonpartisan basis," funding a recall referendum campaign for just one side of the issue is surely a partisan act.[4] The U.S. government has also tried to perpetuate the image of Súmate as a nonpartisan, "respected civic organization committed to promoting free and fair electoral processes and respect for basic rights."[5] State Department "press guidance" sent from Secretary of

State Colin Powell on July 12, 2004, to all U.S. embassies in the Western Hemisphere, including those in Copenhagen, Dublin, Lisbon, London, Madrid, Paris, Rome, The Hague, Tokyo, Geneva, and the intelligence centers in Norfolk, Virginia, Miami and MacDill Air Force Base in Florida, ordered all U.S. representatives to promote the myth of nonpartisan U.S. government funding in Venezuela. The script was laid out as follows:

WHA Press Guidance, July 12, 2004:

Venezuela: Chávez Accusations

Q. Any response to Chávez claims that the U.S. is funding opposition political parties? Is the U.S. funding any part of the election process? If so, how much and to whom?

A: We categorically reject these statements and accusations. This is clearly an attempt to divert attention away from the Venezuelan people's continued efforts to overcome political polarization and reach a constitutional, peaceful, democratic, and electoral solution to the current impasse, in accordance with OAS Resolution 833. . . . The United States provides funding to groups that promote democracy and strengthen civil society in Venezuela. These programs are nonpartisan and open to all parties.[6]

So apparently, the secretary of state considers that organizations that participated in and led to an overthrow of a democratically elected and popularly supported government are merely "promoting democracy and strengthening civil society." The State Department obviously did not reflect on why the April 2002 coup was reversed within 48 hours, nor did they consider the reality of Venezuelan society, where a majority of its people support its democratic government and enjoy the liberties, freedoms, and social guarantees that it provides. In fact, almost none of the groups NED funds in Venezuela truly "promote democracy and strengthen civil society." They all have deep connections to Venezuela's elite and traditional ruling class that lost its power with the Chávez government and has fought bitterly to get it back, even at the risk of violating the constitution and the principles of democracy. Furthermore, none of the programs are nonpartisan, especially considering that the president of NED, Carl Gershman, has publicly declared President Chávez a "dictator." This clearly demonstrates a partisan opinion regarding internal Venezuelan politics that is projected and reflected among NED grantees.

But in the specific case of Súmate, the State Department's statements are ridiculous. How can Súmate's program promote a recall referendum on President Chávez's mandate and remain open to all parties and nonpartisan? By promoting the referendum, Súmate is taking sides, and clearly, those that support the president would not choose to participate in Súmate's campaign.

The U.S. government was well aware that Súmate was born from the extremist opposition movement that executed the April 2002 coup. In a classified cable dated January 2003 sent by U.S. embassy official Frederick Cook to Washington, he wrote, "Opposition will sign up on referendum day: The NGO Súmate is taking the lead in organizing the collection of signatures on what is now being called the 'alternative referendum' scheduled for February 2. . . . Súmate plans to use the day to collect signatures for constitutional mechanisms and to schedule various recall referenda, including: 1) a constitutional amendment, 2) a letter asking Chávez to resign, 3) recall referenda for various Chávista legislators and their alternates, 4) a letter to the international community, and 5) a referendum to abrogate several Chávez-sponsored economic reform laws."[7]

Súmate is an anti-Chávez organization that receives extensive and substantial funding from the United States and is linked to the U.S. government at the highest levels. Súmate "took the lead" in organizing a signature drive for referenda to "ask Chávez to resign," "recall Chávez," "recall various Chavista legislators and their alternates," and "abrogate Chávez-sponsored laws"—clear evidence of their anti-Chávez opposition and partisan position.

As even further evidence of Súmate's partisan status as an opposition political organization, another cable from the U.S. embassy, this time authored by Ambassador Charles Shapiro and sent to Washington in February 2003, revealed: "Planning the Firmazo: Súmate said planning for February 2 began just three and a half weeks ago, when it became apparent that the Supreme Court would strike down the consultative referendum. Working within the DCC [Democratic Coordinator Committee], Súmate argued that the opposition should not simply respond to the disappointment with another march. 'We wanted something tangible, something profound,' [name censored] explained. Once the DCC agreed on the approach, Súmate began work, visiting radio and television stations personally to explain the plan. 'The media embraced the idea, and we got nationwide coverage for the event,' [name censored] said. Súmate expanded its network from approximately 8,000 volunteers in November 2002 to over 270,000 volunteers nationwide."[8]

Let's go back for just a minute and put this into context. It is February 2003, and Venezuela is just coming out of a 64-day lockout and economic sabotage that forced the state oil industry into a severe crisis, resulted in the deaths of dozens of Venezuelans, caused dangerous shortages in food and beverage products. This lockout, or strike, or sabotage, as commonly referred to, was conducted by the same coalition of political parties, social groups, labor unions, business entities, media outlets, and church leaders that had executed the coup against Chávez just ten months before. After the coup, this coalition had come together under the name Democratic Coordinator. The lockout was yet another failure, though it caused more than $10 billion in damages to the national economy and the recall referendum was seen as the next step in the game to remove Chávez from power.[9] The Democratic Coordinator was unquestionably an extremist opposition coalition. Its steering committee, the Democratic Coordinator Committee (DCC), was the high-level group of opposition leaders making decisions regarding actions the opposition would be taking. The cable Ambassador Shapiro sent to Washington clearly states that Súmate was a part of the DCC, and, moreover, that Súmate had a critical role in decision making within that high-level opposition coalition: "Working within the DCC, Súmate argued that the opposition should not simply respond to the disappointment with another march." Furthermore, Súmate was the contact for private media owners, all opposition, and especially at that time, sought to enlist their participation in the next steps to remove President Chávez from power.

So there should be absolutely no question of Súmate's political affiliation. This is not an organization that is dedicated to promoting "election education" for "all Venezuelan citizens." It is an extremist opposition group, funded by the U.S. government and linked to the Bush administration at the highest levels—hence, Machado's one-on-one visit with Bush.

USAID gave Súmate an $84,840 grant in August 2003 for a four-month period through December. That is a lot of money for just four months. These funds were issued from the Office of Transition Initiatives and filtered through its private contractor, Development Alternatives, Inc. This time around, the program had nothing to do with electoral education, but rather aimed at building an "electoral database" and a "communication strategy" for the referendum. Now, why would a non-governmental organization need an "electoral database," unless it was planning on somehow engaging in fraudulent activities with that information? [10]

Súmate even wrote in its quarterly report to NED that it had been using the funding to build a "massive communications strategy" and an "Operations Manual for the 'Reafirmazo.'"[11] Súmate received another $107,200 from NED in 2004 to continue its work in Venezuela on the referendum campaign, and other groups, such as the National Democratic Institute and the International Republican Institute, contributed portions of their more than $3 million in grants during 2004 to aid in Súmate's efforts. Oddly enough, Súmate also received a $300,000 grant from the U.S. Department of Health and Human Services (HHS) to pursue its electoral registry database program. It seems very suspicious that HHS, a health services entity, would fund a foreign organization working in the electoral field. Possibly, HHS was used as another filter for the funding so that it wouldn't be uncovered through Freedom of Information Act requests to NED and USAID. Even stranger is that Súmate's spokesperson, Felix Sánchez, declared to the Venezuelan press that the $300,000 had been returned to HHS because Súmate was unable to complete the project.[12]

Amongst the FOIA documents I received from NED and the State Department were two schedules for visits to Caracas, one for NED president Carl Gershman and the other for a U.S. congressional delegation headed by Representative Cass Ballenger. Besides a lot of uninteresting information about the hotels they stayed in and their flight arrangements, something curious caught my eye. On both of the schedules, the first meeting scheduled in Caracas with any person, group, or government official, including U.S. government officials, was with Súmate. Gershman arrived at approximately 11:38 p.m. in Caracas on November 7, 2004, and his first meeting was scheduled at 8:00 a.m.: "breakfast with Súmate in hotel."[13] On the schedule for Congressman Cass Ballenger, his arrival to Caracas was at 13:30 on August 3, 2004, and his first official meeting was at 16:00 with "Súmate at the Ambassador's residence."[14]

Apparently, Súmate was not only well received by President George W. Bush, but was also considered "top priority" in Caracas. Later down the lists were Venezuelan government officials, including the president and head of Congress, and other figures. Why such special treatment? Possibly because Súmate is and continues to be Washington's main player in Venezuela.

5

Plan Balboa

Plan Balboa, created as a joint military exercise of NATO forces, was carried out in Spain during May 2001. Though this simulated military exercise carries the seal of the armed forces of Spain, neither the Spanish government nor its military play any role in its operation. Plan Balboa specifically involves the nations of Panama, Colombia, Venezuela, and the United States, via its territory of Puerto Rico. Though indicated as a "simulated joint forces military exercise," Plan Balboa differs from other simulations because it contains real satellite images from United States institutions and accurate coordinates of targeted Venezuelan airfields and strategic points within Venezuelan territory. Parts of Plan Balboa are clearly fictitious, such as the description of the internal conflict in Venezuela (described as the "Brown" nation in the original documents from the military exercise) linking it to an anti-Western "terrorist" threat that justifies a fabricated resolution from the United Nations Security Council authorizing military intervention. But many other components of Plan Balboa are based on the reality of the current political environment of the nations involved, particularly between the United States and Venezuela.

Since the creation of Plan Balboa, several actions and measures have been implemented against the "target" nation of Venezuela, though not always in the exact manner as outlined in the simulated operation. Merely eleven months after the Balboa simulation, a coup d'état was executed against the Venezuelan government, supported in large part by the United States, which as the "Blue" nation in the plan played the role of key aggressor against Venezuela. Before, during, and after the April 2002 coup, presence of U.S. military and intelligence equipment and personnel was detected by Venezuelan military intelligence evidencing an intent to engage in military action during the overthrow of President Chávez. In 2005, an international campaign was launched by the United States attempting to link the Venezuelan government to terrorism in order to justify further intervention.[1] Such actions continue to date.

During the first half of 2006, the U.S. government conducted four military exercises in the same "Zone of Operations" as outlined in Plan Balboa. In one of these exercises, "Operation Partnership of the Americas," the U.S. brought four large warships to less than 50 miles off the Venezuelan coast, one of which, the aircraft carrier U.S.S. *George Washington*, held 85 combat planes and 6,500 troops.[2] Other ships, such as the destroyer *Stout*, the *Monterey*, and the *Underwood* carried 300–400 troops each and several Tomahawk missiles and missile launchers. These ships spent nearly a month in the Caribbean basin, launching distance from Venezuela, during a time period when tensions between the two nations had heightened dramatically. At the same time, several other military exercises led by the U.S., such as Joint Caribbean Lion, New Horizons, and Tradewinds, brought in thousands more U.S. forces and heavy-duty, technologically advanced military equipment. A large portion of these exercises were conducted on the island of Curaçao and the other Netherands Antilles. Both Aruba and Curaçao, a mere swim off the coast of Venezuela, house U.S. Air Force bases. The U.S. government has been rapidly expanding its presence in Curaçao during 2006 in an apparent effort to seize military and economic control of the island. More on this will be discussed in chapter 6.

Plan Balboa on its surface appears to be a mere "simulated" invasion plan against Venezuela, but critical incidents during the past few years clearly indicate that many of its components continue to be implemented in an attempt to overthrow the present Venezuelan government. Balboa must be viewed as a "blueprint" of an invasion plan that targets Venezuela.

U.S. Role in Plan Balboa

Though the United States does not appear by name in Plan Balboa, numerous factors indicate that not only is that country the key aggressor in the invasion plan, but that the exercise was developed in the U.S. This is clearly shown through the following:

- The real satellite images included in the "simulated" exercise are taken from a U.S. institution, the Department of Atmospheric Science at the University of Illinois.

- The principal base of operations for the military intervention in Venezuela is Howard Air Force Base, a U.S. base in Panama.

- The satellite image of the "zone of operations" shows the following U.S. territories and areas where U.S. military bases are placed: Guantánamo, Cuba (military base), Puerto Rico (U.S. territory), Panama (large military base), Haiti (U.S. troop presence), Curaçao (FOL base), and Colombia (numerous U.S. military bases and large U.S. troop presence).

- The name of the alleged "anti-Western guerrilla group" that is the target of the military invasion is in English, despite the fact that the exercise was supposedly created in Spain in the Spanish language. The name is Venezuelan Liberation Forces (VLF). Many other abbreviations and indicators in the exercise are also in English.

- The nation labeled as "Blue" fits the characteristics of the United States: Western nation, clearly aligned with Western defense and security organizations; a strong economy with advanced technological industry and petroleum and mining resources, major merchant marine and fishing industry and capacity, territorial waters and islands that border areas of Venezuelan (Brown) territory, provision of material and technical support to Venezuela (Brown) to develop its petroleum industry, strongly allied with the "White" nation (Colombia) and the "Cyan" nation (Panama).

- The Blue nation is placed where the U.S. territory of Puerto Rico is geographically located, though in the Balboa simulation Blue appears much larger in size than Puerto Rico's parameters.

- The fictitious United Nations Security Council resolution authorizing military intervention in Venezuela (Brown) indicates the Blue nation (United States) as the principal provider of military forces in the Joint Combined Allied Force that will carry out the invasion. The U.S. has the largest and most powerful military in the world and traditionally is the principal provider of military forces for joint international interventions (Iraq, Afghanistan, Kosovo, etc.).

- The alleged intervention is justified in order to rescue those citizens of the Blue nation (United States) who are present in the territory of Brown (Venezuela). No other nation is mentioned as the cause for invasion other than Blue, which clearly evidences the power and domination of this nation. Also, the U.S. always uses as an excuse for invasion or direct intervention the "rescue" of its citizens.

- The primary area of invasion in Balboa is labeled as the "Black Zone," which geographically includes the largest developed petroleum resources in Venezuelan territory, in the state of Zulia. This is one of only two states in Venezuela that has an opposition governor, Manuel Rosales, who was the opposition's chosen candidate for the presidency. Rosales has enjoyed overwhelming support from former U.S. Ambassador to Venezuela William Brownfield, who previously ran the U.S. consulate in Zulia State back in 1979. Rosales and his supporters also proposed a separatist agenda for Zulia State, even going so far as to campaign for autonomy from the national government. On a visit to Zulia, Ambassador Brownfield referred to the state as "The Independent Republic of Zulia."[3] The United States has shown unequivocal interest in securing petroleum resources around the world to guarantee a lasting supply for its energy needs. The U.S. utilized a fictitious justification (the presence of weapons of mass destruction) to invade Iraq in 2003 in order to assume control of that nation's vast oil resources. Therefore, it is not unrealistic to speculate that situations such as these could occur in other nations of great oil wealth, such as Venezuela, especially when the region holding the developed oil industry is already in the hands of a U.S. puppet. The deteriorating diplomatic relationship between the U.S. and Venezuela has caused concern in some U.S. political circles regarding Venezuela as a reliable supplier of oil. Additionally, as has been shown in the pre-

ceding chapters , intervention in Venezuela to remove its present government from power has been suggested by several conservative think
tanks and members of the U.S. government during the past few years.

From Balboa to the Present Political Environment

Plan Balboa's general concept is a semi-fictitious situation that mirrors the
United States vision of Venezuela's political climate. According to the simulation, the political situation in Venezuela (Brown) has deteriorated and
its "radical and nationalist" political party, "PPL," has threatened to take
hostile actions against Blue's fishing fleets. The VLF "anti-Western guerrilla group," aligned with the PPL, controls the Black Zone (developed oil
industry) in Venezuela and is supported by the population. The VLF also
controls the military in the Black Zone and the aerial bases and equipment.
The VLF/PPL have threatened the lives of citizens of Blue country (U.S.)
that live in Venezuela (Brown) and Blue's economic interests. The possibility exists that parties from third nations (probably Cuba and Colombian
guerrillas) will join together with the VLF forces against Blue. Colombia
(White) has offered its airfields and military bases in Cartagena, Soledad,
and Bolivar to Blue for its operations. Panama (Cyan) has approved the use
of Howard Air Force Base for Blue's military deployment. The VLF has
threatened to destroy petroleum resources in Venezuela if its installations
are attacked.

- No such political parties as indicated in Plan Balboa exist in
  Venezuela; the PPL is clearly meant to represent the current government party, MVR, led by President Hugo Chávez, that has leftist and
  nationalist tendencies. Also, there are no recognized "guerrilla
  groups" in Venezuela such as the VLF, but for the purposes of Plan
  Balboa, the VLF could represent the radical wing of the MVR, or
  those who support Venezuela's leftist president, Hugo Chávez. Plan
  Balboa intentionally distorts Venezuela's political reality for the purposes of the simulated military invasion because technically a United
  Nations Security Council resolution authorizing military intervention
  could not easily be obtained against a member nation with a democrat-

ic government, such as Venezuela's present government. Therefore, for the effectiveness of the simulation, the situation in Venezuela had to be altered, so that it appeared as though the radical or "leftist" elements in Venezuela were not in power in the government, but rather comprised "guerrilla groups" threatening the fictitious Brown country and economic and human interests of allied nations.

- The United States has attempted to portray Venezuela's President Chávez and his supporters as "anti-American" and allied with "terrorists" and "guerrilla groups" in Colombia (FARC and ELN) and others throughout the region, as well as in the Middle East. In Plan Balboa, the VLF is considered as "anti-Western" (read anti-American) and aligned with guerrilla groups in neighboring Colombia (White). The parallel here is undeniable.

- Plan Balboa claims the political situation in Venezuela/Brown has deteriorated. Blue repeatedly claims that the Chávez government threatens Brown's democracy, as well as regional stability and security, and that the internal situation is in crisis as a result of Chávez's politics and alleged human rights violations.

- Plan Balboa claims that the VLF controls the military and threatens economic interests of Blue, specifically oil supply. The VLF has threatened to sabotage petroleum installations in the case of invasion. In reality, the Chávez government has the loyalty of its armed forces and has stated that in the event of a U.S. invasion in Venezuelan territory, oil supply will be terminated. In recent times, President Chávez has gone further to state that were the U.S. to invade the country, the oil fields would be blown up by government loyalists. The U.S. Congress has already commissioned reports to determine the dependence on Venezuelan oil and has ordered the preparation of contingency plans to lessen the impact were such a scenario to take place.[4]

- Balboa presents Brown as a nation in conflict threatening the region in a way that raises cause for a combined forces intervention authorized by the United Nations. In reality, the United States is seeking avenues in the United Nations to pursue sanctions against the Venezuelan government and resolutions that could lead to future interventions in Venezuela.

Manifestations of Plan Balboa in Venezuela

- Eleven months after the Plan Balboa exercises, the coup took place in Venezuela. Evidence shows the presence of U.S. warships and submarines off the coast of Venezuelan territory during the days before and during the coup. U.S. special forces and military intelligence were in continuous contact with Venezuelans involved in the coup in the months preceding and during it. Authorization requests were made by U.S. military forces to transport unusual military equipment into Venezuelan territory in the days preceding the coup and the presence of Blackhawk helicopters and other planes owned by the U.S. military was detected during that same period.[5]

- The United States continues to make concerted efforts to link President Chávez and his supporters to terrorist groups, including FARC and ELN from Colombia, and even groups such as Hezbollah and al-Qaeda. Such efforts are destined to justify international intervention in Venezuela in order to remove its current administration, which has demonstrated opposition to U.S. foreign policy in Latin America and other parts of the world.

- The United States has launched an international propaganda campaign attempting to portray President Chávez as "undemocratic," a "dictator," a "terrorist supporter," and a "threat to democracy in the region." The United States has hinted at efforts to invoke the Charter of the Organization of American States in order to intervene legally in Venezuela to "restore" democracy. Efforts are presently being made in the United Nations to similar effect.

- The U.S. government has funneled millions of dollars of aid to opposition groups in Venezuela, many of which participated in the coup in April 2002 and have engaged in other illegal and undemocratic activities during the past few years, such as the oil industry sabotage and violent actions in the streets intended to destabilize the nation.

- The *Washington Post* affirmed in November 2005 that the Pentagon has developed an invasion plan for Venezuela as part of the latest Quadrennial Defense Review and in accordance with the March 2005 National Defense Strategy of the United States. The plan targets Venezuela as an "irregular threat" requiring an "asymmetric warfare plan." Venezuela is presently viewed by the Department of Defense as a "hostile" and "unstable" nation.[6]

- Unprecedented military exercises have been conducted off the coast of Venezuela during the first half of 2006. Four U.S. military-run operations were in place at the same time, all in the Caribbean basin, two of which were specifically based out of Curaçao in the neighboring Netherands Antilles. One of the exercises, as mentioned above, Operation Partnership of the Americas, brought in four huge warships carrying on board more than 8,000 troops, numerous Tomahawk missiles and missile launchers, and 85 combat planes. The U.S.S. *George Washington*, one of the Pentagon's largest aircraft carriers, spent approximately one month floating around near the Venezuelan coast, with a clear launching distance for any of its F-16 fighter jets. Another exercise, Operation New Horizons, brought 3,500 troops to the Dominican Republic in late April 2006 as part of a four-month "humanitarian and training mission." The presence of Blackhawk helicopters and armored vehicles raised suspicions that the U.S. military was on more than just a humanitarian mission. The *Los Angeles Times* reported that radio broadcasts in the Dominican Republic claimed 11,000 more U.S. troops would soon arrive on the island. The Dominican Republic is just a short trip off the Venezuelan coast.[7]

- In April 2006, Director of National Intelligence John Negroponte admitted that the U.S. military had sent a nuclear submarine to intercept communications off the coast of Venezuela. The submarine, U.S.S. *Virginia*, spent more than 90 days navigating in the Caribbean in late 2005 on its espionage mission. Negroponte stated that such an exercise was part of a larger strategy to "strengthen our presence and operations in places where we haven't been recently, where we have let things go since the Cold War, such as Latin America and Africa."[8]

- In the state of Zulia in western Venezuela, the site of the invasion in Plan Balboa, a recent separatist movement calls for autonomy from the national government. "Zulia First" is the slogan of the state's governor, Manuel Rosales, one of only two opposition governors in the country, out of 23 states. Rosales was the opposition's chosen "unity" candidate during the 2006 presidential elections. He enjoyed a close relationship with Ambassador William Brownfield, who served as the

U.S. consul in Zulia back in 1979. Brownfield made frequent trips to Zulia and publicly declared his approval of an "independent republic of Zulia." In Balboa, the state of Zulia is the only area officially "occupied" by the international forces involved in the invasion. Were the state to become "separate" or "autonomous" from the rest of the country, the principal goal of Plan Balboa would be achieved.

Plan Balboa was clearly developed as a blueprint invasion operation targeting Venezuela. When Plan Balboa is viewed in light of developments that have threatened the stability of Venezuela's democratic and popularly supported government led by President Chávez, it becomes clear that the operation is an outline for what those individuals, groups, and governments intent on subverting the will of Venezuela's majority plan to do. There is no doubt that the United States is present in Plan Balboa, despite its clever but *superficial* exclusion from the documents.

6

Curaçao: The Third Frontier of the United States

Tropical breezes, calm, warm ocean waters, beaming sunshine and mellow attitudes— these envelope the Caribbean island of Curaçao. With less than 180,000 inhabitants and a land area of merely 177 square miles, Curaçao forms part of the Netherlands Antilles, one of three self-governing divisions of the Kingdom of the Netherlands. The other two are the Netherlands and Aruba. The Netherands Antilles are composed of five islands: Bonaire, Curaçao, Saba, St. Maarten, and St. Eustatius. Curaçao is largest and most populated, and hosts the main government that oversees the other islands. Curaçao has one of the largest natural ports in the world, with deep waters right off its coasts and long landscapes perfect for the docking of large ships. The island's principal industries are its oil refinery and tourism. The refinery, owned by the Curaçao government, has been leased to Venezuela's state oil company, PDVSA, since 1984. It is a large refinery with vast capacities to process different types of crude oil, from the lightest and sweetest to the heaviest and thickest.

The people of Curaçao are a multicultural mix of polyglots, with a majority of Afro-Caribbean descent. Almost all citizens speak at least four languages: the native Papiamento, Dutch, English, and Spanish. There are significant social movements on the island that seek recuperation of the majority's African heritage and independence from the Dutch kingdom. Curaçao is located less than fifty miles off the coast of Venezuela and shares a rich history with its South American neighbor. Curaçao native Pedro Luís Brión fought alongside liberator Simón Bolivar in the 1800s to free Venezuela from Spanish colonial rule. Curaçao shares important social and economic trade and exchanges with Venezuela, aside from the oil refinery. The only truly fresh fruits and vegetables available in Curaçao arrive on small boats from Venezuela every few days and are sold at the floating market in the capital city of Willemstad.

Curaçao also happens to be fertile ground for one of the U.S. military's largest forward operating locations (FOLs) in the region. A forward operating location is a small air base maintained by the U.S. military that is used for monitoring and combating drug trafficking activities and as platforms for counter-narcotics flights. The FOLs were established by formal agreement with the governments of Curaçao and Aruba, where another small FOL is located, Ecuador (in Manta, where a fairly large base functions), and El Salvador (in Comalapa, which houses an operative cell) after the official closure of Howard Air Force Base in Panama, which previously had served as the main base for counter-narcotics activities and U.S. military actions in the region. In Curaçao, the FOL is located on the grounds of Hato International Airport, and it shares a large extension with the Dutch government's air base. Officially, the FOL in Curaçao "supports two large, two medium and six small aircraft, with as many as 200 to 230 temporarily deployed operations and maintenance personnel. The Curaçao site is currently hosting Air National Guard F-16s, Navy P-3 and E-2 Airborne Early Warning planes, U.S. Air Force E-3 AWACS and other U.S. aircraft."[1]

Despite this permanent U.S. military presence right off the coast of Venezuela, the Venezuelan government had not considered Curaçao an area of geopolitical strategic importance, nor as a threat until February 27, 2005, when a major U.S. warship, the U.S.S. *Saipan,* spontaneously and with no notice given to the Venezuelan government as protocol requires, docked in the large port of Caracas Bay. On board were more than 1,400 marines and 35 helicopters. The *Saipan,* termed "America's Top Gator," is "designed to put troops on hostile shores, serving as a primary landing ship for assault operations of Marine expeditionary units. Assaults are carried out by landing craft and helicopters. In a secondary role, *Saipan* also performs sea control and power projection missions. Her purpose is to sail in harm's way and provide a rapid buildup of combat power ashore in the face of opposition. The United States maintains the largest and most capable amphibious force in the world, and *Saipan* sails proudly on its front line."[2]

The *Saipan*'s last operation prior to its clandestine Caribbean mission was in support of Operation Enduring Iraqi Freedom in 2003. The ship has a troop capacity of over 1,800 and a crew of a little more than 1,000. It can carry 200 amphibious vehicles, up to 35 helicopters, and 7 landing craft. Onboard armament includes an SWY-2 Ship Self-Defense System with two RAM GMLS, two Phalanx Close-in Weapons Systems, three .50-caliber gun mounts, and six .25mm chain guns.

So when the U.S.S. *Saipan* just appeared without notice off the coast of Venezuela, the Venezuelan government and military took it as a sign of intimidation, if not a direct threat. U.S. Ambassador William Brownfield declared to the press that the reason notice had not been given about the *Saipan*'s proximity was due to a "lack of communication." Brownfield blamed the failure in communication on the fact that the Venezuelan minister of defense and commander of the armed forces had not yet formally received him in official meetings. Funny, the Venezuelan ambassador had been in Washington for more than three years and had never met with either the U.S. secretary of defense or the chief of the armed forces. It wasn't until 2006, three years after he arrived in Washington as Venezuela's ambassador, that he was finally granted a meeting with an assistant secretary of state. The secretary of state has never offered to meet with Ambassador Bernardo Alvarez in Washington, yet Ambassador William Brownfield in Venezuela felt entitled to be received by the highest levels of the Venezuelan government. "I regret that I have not yet had the pleasure to meet and speak with the Minister of Defense or the commander of the Armed Forces or any other functionary of the Venezuelan Armed Forces," Brownfield declared in early March 2005, noting that "if I had spoken with them I'd have told them the date of the arrival of the [*Saipan*] . . . . The truth is," Brownfield added, "it is our desire to have more visits by ships to Curaçao and Aruba over the coming weeks, months and years."[3]

And so it was.

Though the remainder of 2005 saw few U.S. warships docking in Curaçao, 2006 made up for the previous year's low U.S. military presence. When the international press began reporting that the U.S. military would be conducting major exercises and operations in the Caribbean region with legions of warships, marines, combat planes and helicopters beginning in March 2006, it drew attention in Venezuela. The military exercises, New Horizons 2006 and Tradewinds 2006, taking place in El Salvador, Honduras, the Dominican Republic, and Jamaica, did not signal serious concern, since their primary focus was humanitarian in nature and, in the case of Tradewinds, preparation for the World Cricket Cup to be held in Jamaica during 2006. But Operation Partnership of the Americas raised eyebrows. Beginning in April 2006, Partnership of the Americas was slated to last from April to June and bring in a major wartime aircraft carrier, the U.S.S. *George Washington*, along with its strike group of three other warships, the destroyer *Stout*, the guided-missile cruiser *Monterey*, and the frigate *Underwood*.

Partnership of the Americas was to be based around the Netherands Antilles, with particular emphasis on Curaçao, where all of the ships would eventually dock or pass through at some point during the mission. The *George Washington* was carrying 6,500 marines, plus a few hundred crew, and 85 combat planes, including F-14D Tomcats, F/A-18 Hornets, S-3A/B Vikings, E-2C Hawkeyes, EA-6B Prowlers, and Seahawk helicopters. Along with the other three ships, the combined total troop presence was near 8,000.[4]

The U.S. government said the exercise was "routine," yet the U.S. military hasn't conducted military operations of this size in the Caribbean region since the Cold War. Venezuela had a logical reason to be alarmed. The military buildup was occurring at the beginning of a major election year in Venezuela (presidential elections in December), U.S. verbal hostilities were at an all-time high, the State and Defense Departments were attempting to link the Venezuelan government with terrorist groups, and Venezuela was about to be sanctioned by the Bush administration for allegedly "not cooperating with counter-narcotics activities" and for "not fully cooperating with the war on terrorism." Furthermore, Operation Partnership of the Americas was aimed at preparing for a "possible terrorist threat" in the region, or a "threat to regional security." These are terms the U.S. is quick to apply to nations that don't serve its interests. And to top it all off, William Brownfield was the only U.S. ambassador in the region to make an official visit aboard the U.S.S. *George Washington* before it departed Florida.

U.S. Ambassador to Venezuela William Brownfield in fighter gear,
coming off of the U.S.S. *George Washington* aircraft carrier before its commencement
of Operation Partnership of the Americas, April 9, 2006.

As the warships approached Curaçao, I decided to check out the scene on the island. Despite Curaçao's desert beauty, the situation on one of the closest and most strategic nations for Venezuela was quite worrisome.

When I arrived to Curaçao in mid-April, the destroyer *Stout* had just left the docks in Willemstad, and the town was buzzing with talk about the presence of major U.S. warships around their island at a time of high tensions with Venezuela. The *Stout* had actually conducted its "change of command" ceremony at the Mega-Pier dock in Willemstad, though rather unusual for a U.S. warship to host such a ceremony on foreign territory. In the presence of Curaçao's prime minister Emily Jongh-Elhage and local press, Commander Thomas K. Kiss assumed his new position as the ship's leader, stating, the U.S.S. *Stout* "has a formidable presence to defend U.S. interests in the region." Commander Kiss later proclaimed to the Curaçao press, "We are the most powerful naval force in the world and we will defend our friends in the region under all circumstances."

A subsequent article on April 11, 2006, in Curaçao's *La Prensa,* said, "The journalists selected to go on board the *Stout* did not dare to ask the question that everyone wanted to ask: Does the presence of this ship here have anything to do with the latest developments regarding Venezuela? Not even Curaçao's press bought the storyline from Washington that claimed the ship was visiting for some R&R [rest and recreation]. We have heard that argument before, but there are few who believe that these visits are just about some good R&R. This military officer in charge of this ship that monitors all directions is looking right at Venezuela." [5]

The same article in Curaçao's local press went on to mention, "The *Stout*'s visit to Curaçao was accompanied by Jane Akkers, author of the famous essay published by the State Department, 'The Third Frontier of the United States,' which proposes the islands of Curaçao, Bonaire and Aruba form part of the geopolitical border of the United States."[6]

Third frontier of the United States? It may sound absurd to some, since the "ABC" islands form part of the Dutch kingdom and are legally not U.S. territory, but strategically it is clearly in the interests of the U.S. government to dominate that area primarily because of its proximity to Venezuela's wealthy oil fields. And this is precisely what the U.S. is pursuing on the ground, in real time, in Curaçao and Aruba.

Most of the islanders I met were anxious to talk about the growing U.S. presence on the island and the fear that Curaçao could become a launching point for an attack on Venezuela. I received information from various different sources, and all of it matched and was also corroborated by press reports, so I don't doubt its veracity. The U.S. has been spreading its economic and military influence all over Curaçao. Aruba is already in the hands of U.S. corporations and government-related industries. The oil refinery in Aruba is owned by the Valero Energy Corporation, a San Antonio, Texas, oil company with close ties to the Bush family, and is known to have the largest refining capacity in North America. According to several sources in Curaçao, Valero has been actively pressuring the Curaçao government and its state oil company, Refineria do Kurosu (RDK), to break its leasing contract with PDVSA and sell the refinery to Valero. PDVS's current contract with RDK is good through 2019, but Valero apparently has made an offer to pay all damages related to liquidating the contract. If Valero were to buy out the Curaçao refinery, the U.S. would have a hold on major Caribbean oil refineries that service the Central American and Caribbean regions. Obviously, the oil that is processed in the Curaçao refinery comes from Venezuela, and it may not be made available were the refinery to fall into the hands of a U.S. corporation. However, the move by Valero to take control over the Curaçao refinery appears to be part of a larger strategy to remove Venezuelan interests from the island and to gain geopolitical control over the zone. This is a longer-term goal.

Apart from the refinery, U.S. companies and government-related business associates have already either completely bought out or bought significant shares of several strategic companies in Curaçao —all during 2006. These companies include:

- ENNIA, the largest insurance company on the island,

- The water and electricity company, Aqualectra, which has the highest prices in the world

- Banco del Caribe, the most important and powerful bank on the island

- Curinfo, the digital communications company that controls internet and digital phone access

- Hotel Van der Walk Plaza, which historically has been the most prestigious hotel in Curaçao

(Note: The U.S. government has also leased the majority of space in the Holiday Beach Hotel, with neighboring restaurant Denny's, to give it a "homey" feeling. This is where the U.S. military houses its personnel.) Water, electricity, internet, digital phone, banks, insurance, hotels—these are all entities that control the basic infrastructure of the island. By owning and controlling the infrastructure and the oil refinery, and expanding already authorized military operations, the U.S. is rapidly achieving its geopolitical goal of dominating the island. Furthermore, most islanders confirmed the rumor that the U.S. military is seeking to expand its FOL operations to include a naval base. And corroborating Ambassador Brownfield's statement, that the U.S. plans to have more visits of its warships to Curaçao over the coming months and years, the Curaçao Port Authority confirmed that the U.S. has requested clearance for more than a hundred warships to enter its port and territory during the year 2006.[7] According to Port Authority officials, the normal requests in prior years have been for no more than ten warships annually. The jump to a hundred is a significant and alarming increase that causes one to question why the U.S. would need to bring so many warships into the zone, unless it was planning on invading a nearby country.

In June 2006, the U.S. and its NATO partners conducted Operation Joint Caribbean Lion. This time around, U.S. and NATO forces physically took over the island and assumed control of Curaçao's communications towers, hospitals, government buildings, and other strategic installations during an exercise. But the exercise had a curious goal: to capture the rebel terrorist leader, "Hugo Le Grande" (Hugo the Grand). Could there be any implication of intent in the choice of the name Hugo?

Right-wing factions in the Dutch government and throughout Curaçao have launched a campaign to convince the islanders that President Chávez is the one who wants to "invade" Curaçao, Aruba, and Bonaire. One Curaçao paper, the *De Groene Amsterdammer*, used the headline "Chávez Is a Virus" and reinforced the unsubstantiated claim that Chávez wants to "invade" the islands. Despite absolutely no evidence to show that President Chávez has ever made such statements, the conservative press in Curaçao has bombarded its citizens with propaganda attempting to raise fears about Chávez's intentions. Holland's minister of defense, Henk Kamp, declared in April 2006, "Chávez shows ambitions toward those small territories situated north of the Venezuelan coast and that form part of the Dutch Kingdom."[8] Such statements appear to have been made to justify the heightened U.S. military presence on the islands, since no visible or invisible Venezuelan threat had ever been made against the Netherands Antilles.

The people of Curaçao are steadfast on not allowing their island to become a launching pad for U.S. aggression in the region. Many are outright opposed to the U.S. military base and the growing U.S. ownership of the island's infrastructure. Yet the actions being taken by the U.S. government and its associates appear to be beyond the control of the locals. The little island of Curaçao, home to that lovely blue liqueur and warm people, has now been caught in the middle of a growing conflict between two great regional powers.

7

A Note on Asymmetric War and Wizard's Chess

The three major fronts of attack the U.S. government has been employing against Venezuela during the past few years form part of an asymmetric war. "War as a whole," "war of all the people," contemporary nontraditional, fourth-generation or irregular war, are some of the other terms used to describe this nonconventional conflict where the battlefield is extended to everyone and everywhere.[1] The conflict may be "military or nonmilitary, lethal or nonlethal, or a mix of everything within a state's or a coalition of states' array of instruments of power. As such, it may be a zero-sum game in which only one winner emerges, or in a worst-case scenario, no winner."[2]

In asymmetric war, there are no rules, nothing is forbidden; it is warfare in the age of globalization. Some military experts refer to asymmetric war as a fourth-generation conflict, which uses the disparity between the contending parties to gain advantage. First- through third-generation conflicts include more traditional types of military engagements, from "low-tech attrition war" (the more opponents killed, the better) to "outperforming war" (employ speed, surprise, and lethality to hit an enemy's weak spots), to the employment of "brainpower" to achieve success against an enemy.[3] Fourth-generation war employs the use of "strategic asymmetry," defined as "acting, organizing and thinking differently than opponents in order to maximize one's own advantages, exploit an opponent's weaknesses, attain the initiative, or gain greater freedom of action. It can have both psychological and physical dimensions."[4] Experts such as Colonel Max G. Manwaring of the U.S. Army (Retired) believe that fourth-generation conflict is a "methodology the weak employ against the strong," but in Washington's war on Venezuela, strategic asymmetry appears to be the choice modus operandi.[5]

In Colonel Manwaring's "Venezuela's Hugo Chávez, Bolivarian Socialism and Asymmetric Warfare," written for and published by the Institute for Strategic Studies of the U.S. Army in October 2005, President Chávez is referred to as a "wise competitor" who "will not even attempt to defeat his enemies on their terms. Rather, he will seek to shift the playing field away from conventional military confrontations and turn to nontraditional forms of assault on a nation's stability and integrity. Thus, it appears that this astute warrior is prepared to destabilize, to facilitate the processes of state failure, and thus to 'destroy in order to rebuild' in true revolutionary fashion."[6] Interestingly, Colonel Manwaring refers to Venezuela's political system, "bolivarianism," as a type of "people's democracy," which he also categorizes together with "dysfunctional, rogue, criminal and narco-states" that "endanger global security, peace and prosperity."[7] So now "people's democracies" are considered criminal and terrorist in the eyes of the U.S. military.

Manwaring, who claims Chávez pursues "all means from propaganda to terrorism to drug trafficking to total destruction of a targeted society" to accomplish his goals, recommends "a coherent, patient action that encompasses all agencies of a targeted government and its international allies. That kind of action would include the fields of politics, diplomacy, defense, intelligence, law enforcement and economic and social development."[8] In other words, basically everything the U.S. government is currently doing to Venezuela.

Actions have already been taken in the political and diplomatic fields, as outlined in chapters 1 and 2 of this book. The defense, intelligence, and law enforcement angles are shown through invasion threats, military buildup, strategic geopolitical maneuvers and psychological warfare (discussed in chapters 5, 6, and 8). And in the economic and social development arena, the sanctions the U.S. government has placed on Venezuela for allegedly, though not actually, failing to collaborate with the efforts against drug trafficking, terrorism, and trafficking in persons have an economic effect, while efforts to finance the Venezuelan opposition have a social impact (chapters 3 and 4). Therefore, it is evident that Colonel Manwaring's "Doctrine of Asymmetric War Against Venezuela" is currently being implemented.

Manwaring admits that asymmetric war is "the only kind of war the United States has ever lost."[9] He indicates that Chávez is provoking a "Super Insurgency" throughout the region, which is resonating with large numbers of people in Venezuela and Latin America, and must be viewed as a form of "Wizard's Chess."[10] Considering Chávez a "true and wise enemy" who must be dealt with by implementing a strategic-level, multidimensional, and multinational paradigm for contemporary asymmetric conflict, Colonel Manwaring recommends a "unified civil-military" response that understands the "fundamental nature of subversion and insurgency" and the ways in which "political-psychological considerations affect the use of force." He particularly suggests using "local and global media" and an "intelligence capability several steps beyond the present norm" in order to compete with Chávez.[11] Clearly, the U.S. has already been implementing such measures. The international propaganda campaign against Chávez is in full swing as is the new special CIA mission destined to focus only on Venezuela and Cuba.

"Wizard's Chess" is right out of *Harry Potter,* but Colonel Manwaring utilizes the concept to demonstrate the type of war Washington is engaging in with Venezuela. He summarizes "the deadly game of 'Wizard's Chess' as a metaphorical example of contemporary asymmetric conflict. . . . In the game, protagonists move pieces silently and subtly all over the game board. Under the players' studied direction, each piece represents a different type of direct and indirect power and might simultaneously conduct its lethal and nonlethal attacks from differing directions. Each piece shows no mercy against its foe and is prepared to sacrifice itself in order to allow another piece the opportunity to destroy or control an adversary—or checkmate the king. Over the long term, however, this game is not a test of expertise in creating instability, conducting illegal violence, or achieving commercial, ideological, or moral satisfaction. Ultimately, it is an exercise in survival. Failure in Wizard's Chess is not an option."[12]

The U.S. government never sees failure as an option, and as has been shown through centuries of invasions and interventions around the world, it will continue and repeat, and sometimes improve, its efforts until its goal is achieved. Wizard's Chess against Chávez began more than four years ago, and so far, the U.S. is losing. It failed in the coup attempt, the economic sabotage or "lockout" and the recall referendum—the three previous stages of intervention. But now the stakes are higher and the stronger pieces are being put into place to make their move.

The Pentagon recently finalized its "most ambitious plan yet" to fight terrorism around the world. Though details of the plan are secret, the military's role is expanded, particularly in the area of elite special operations troops, to be employed outside the war zones of Afghanistan and Iraq. The Special Operations Command of the Pentagon, based in Tampa, Florida, has already dispatched "small teams of Army Green Berets and other Special Operations troops to U.S. Embassies in about 20 countries in the Middle East, Asia, Africa and Latin America, where they are doing operational planning and intelligence gathering to enhance the ability to conduct military operations where the United States is not at war."[13] There is no doubt that Venezuela is one of the countries where elite Special Forces have been "dispatched." Just what kind of military operations are being planned by the U.S. in Venezuela is unclear, but what can be guaranteed is that the game of Wizard's Chess is not yet over. Will the elite forces move in to take out Venezuela's "king," or will the Bolivarian Revolution truly aid in bringing about, as President Chávez has declared, "the end of U.S. imperialism" in this century? What can be assured is that neither side will stop, be it on the defense or the offense, until the final "Checkmate!" is declared.

8

Psyop War

"Psychological operations [psyops] are planned operations to convey selected information and indicators to foreign audiences to influence the emotions, motives, objective reasoning and ultimately the behavior of foreign governments, organizations, groups and individuals. Psyops are a vital part of the broad range of U.S. diplomatic, informational, military, and economic activities."[1] So begins the latest version of the "Doctrine for Joint Psychological Operations of the U.S. Department of Defense."[2] Psyops are used to induce or reinforce the attitudes and behavior of persons and governments in a way that is favorable to the originator's objective. The Pentagon does not just utilize psyops during wartime, but also uses them against friendly nations during peacetime to "inform and influence," as well as to lower "adversary morale" and "create dissidence and disaffection within the ranks."[3] There are three categories of psyops currently employed by the U.S. military: strategic psyops, which include the international information activities conducted by U.S. government agencies, such as USAID, NED, State Department, CIA, and others, to influence foreign attitudes, perceptions, and behavior favorable to the goals and objectives of the U.S. in times of peace and conflict; operational psyops, which are military operations conducted even during peacetime to promote an effective military campaign and strategy; and tactical psyops, which support tactical military missions against opposing forces.[4]

In the case of Venezuela, the main categories of psyops employed are strategic and operational. On a semi-public scale, psyops are conducted by the State Department's outlets in Venezuela, such as the U.S. embassy, USAID, and NED grantees, and other related entities. The CIA and the Defense Intelligence Agency are also quite active in propaganda campaigns and manipulating public opinion in Venezuela, though these tactics are often harder to uncover. One psyops campaign was discovered in the barracks of Venezuela's armed forces during 2005—flyers that read "People of Venezuela: This is the AK-103 rifle used by international terrorist movements and acquired on Tuesday, May 17, 2005, by the regime. of Hugo Chávez Frías. . . . With this rifle, our armed forces become an undercover instrument at the service of guerrilla groups and international terrorism. . . . With this rifle, Fidel Castro shot thousands of Cubans who opposed his miserable communist regime. . . . With this rifle, Hugo Chávez threatens the people of Venezuela today with a false message of peace, in order to subject them to his revolutionary-nationalist-socialist-fascist and totalitarian regime."[5]

Another flyer, discovered passing through military bases and camps, called for insurrection among the ranks: "Venezuelan Soldier: Resist . . . Reject the militarization of Venezuelan society . . . Don't let yourself be manipulated by lies disguised as truth . . . The only invasion is the Castro-communist Cuban regime's invasion . . . that has been lying to its people for more than 46 years about a false 'imperialist Yankee' invasion . . . Venezuelans are democrats . . . For our history, for Bolívar, and by conviction!!! Reject the misery, the hatred and the killer rifles of international terrorism . . . We don't want the Yankee invasion that we have never had . . . But we certainly don't want the Castro-communist Cuban invasion that we are living . . . !! Reject the invaders with bravery . . . !! NO to interventionism! No to disrespecting our sovereignty!"[6]

These types of propaganda campaigns represent classical psyops conducted by special U.S. military intelligence teams. In this case, the campaign was directed at Venezuela's armed forces, primarily lower-ranking soldiers, and attempted to influence their perception of the new defense equipment purchased by the government. The psyops campaigns in Venezuela have focused on dividing sectors within the armed forces and promoting disloyalty to the government.

Just a few months earlier, the Pentagon's Special Operations Command (USSOCOM) established the Joint Psychological Operations Support Element (JPOSE), also referred to as "Gypsy," an elite team of "psychological warriors" that assists psyops personnel stationed at military headquarters overseas. Gypsy is directed by Colonel James A. Treadwell, whose prior psyops gig was in Iraq in 2003, where he was chief of the 4th Psychological Operations Group during the U.S. invasion. He also ran a similar team in Afghanistan in 2001. With a $77.5 million budget for the next six years, Gypsy has a team of more than 38 psyops experts, 113 military forces, and several graphic artists and videographers. In 2005, USSOCOM deployed these specialized Gypsy teams throughout Latin America, the Middle East, and other strategic regions, particularly focusing on Venezuela and Bolivia in the Western Hemisphere.[7]

The 4th Psychological Operations Group that Colonel Treadwell ran in Iraq is the same group that previously staffed the National Security Council's Office of Public Diplomacy (OPD), responsible for illegally planting stories in the U.S. media to favorably portray the Reagan administration's backing of the counterrevolutionary (Contras) forces in Nicaragua. The OPD was shut down in 1987 after the General Accounting Office issued a report confirming that the office, under the reign of anti-Castro Cuban-American Otto Reich, had engaged in unlawful activities by planting "black propaganda" in U.S. media. The OPD filtered stories into the *Washington Post, New York Times* and *Wall Street Journal* that praised U.S. policy and denigrated the Sandinista government as "terrorist," "anti-democratic," and "dangerous." [8]

In more recent years, the Pentagon's Office of Strategic Influence (OSI) has been exposed for paying journalists to write for websites and other news outlets that it sponsors in order to influence public opinion and policymakers.[9] OSI was created right after the September 11, 2001, attacks in the United States as a coordinating entity for psyops in the Middle East. OSI was also allegedly discovered "developing plans to provide news items, possibly even false ones, to foreign media organizations" in an effort to promote and justify U.S. actions in the Middle East.[10] U.S. law prohibits the government from officially using propaganda tactics and psyops within the United States, but the OSI and other psyops campaigns conducted abroad are easily picked up by U.S. news outlets and filtered into national media. This appears to be the case with regard to Venezuela.

In order to try to avoid public scrutiny and make its operations harder to detect, the Pentagon contracted three private corporations for over $300 million to aid in "injecting more creativity" into its psychological operation campaigns over five years. Colonel James Treadwell indicated that the private companies would enable the U.S. military to use "cutting-edge types of media," including radio and television spots, documents, text messages, pop-up ads on the internet, podcasting, billboards, and novelty items.[11] The three contracts were awarded to major defense contractors, SYColeman, Inc., Lincoln Group, and Science Applications International Corp. (SAIC).

SAIC's Venezuela Connection

Of these three U.S. companies, Science Applications International Corp. has a particular history with Venezuela, and not a nice one. SAIC, though headquartered in San Diego, has more than 16,000 employees in the Washington region, and is one of the Pentagon's largest contractors. It is presently completing a $100 billion modernization effort for the U.S. Army and previously created a digital case-management system for the Federal Bureau of Investigation. SAIC's board of directors includes former Joint Chiefs of Staff, ex-CIA officials, and former high-level U.S. government employees. In 1995, SAIC entered into a joint venture with Venezuela's state oil company, PDVSA, to create the information and technology enterprise INTESA. This company, 60 percent owned by SAIC and 40 percent by PDVSA, was responsible for updating and digitalizing old analog systems in the oil industry and, by 1998, completely controlled all the electronic operations at PDVSA. Referred to as "the brain of PDVSA," INTESA used its all-encompassing power in December 2002 to sabotage the equipment and networks necessary to run the industry in collaboration with the opposition's imposed strike, which was intended to force President Chávez, once again, from power. From remote locations, INTESA employees altered access codes and programming, making it impossible for remaining

PDVSA workers to run computers, machines, and refinery equipment. As a result, Venezuela's oil production was brought to a halt and the economic losses were devastating. Not only were common Venezuelans denied gas and oil, but Venezuela's contracts with international partners were threatened severely.

Though PDVSA's president at the time, Alí Rodriguéz, tried to amicably resolve the conflict with INTESA, the info-tech company refused to stop the sabotage and even rejected pleas to hand over passwords, codes, and access keys that would enable loyal PDVSA employees to get the industry off the ground. Eventually, PDVSA had no choice but to enter INTESA headquarters and take over operations. The strike and sabotage eventually failed, but damage had been done to the oil industry that cost Venezuela a near economic depression. SAIC later sued PDVSA, claiming INTESA had been unlawfully expropriated, and in a partisan hearing conducted by the Overseas Protection for International Companies (OPIC), a U.S. government agency that insures U.S. corporations abroad, SAIC won $6 million in damages from PDVSA.[12]

And now SAIC appears on the scene again, working to destabilize Venezuela through multimillion-dollar Pentagon contracts to devise psyops campaigns. SAIC certainly knows the terrain well.

International Psyops Campaign

The media war within Venezuela began several months before the April 2002 coup and hasn't let up much since then. The four private television stations with national broadcast reach, Globovisión, RCTV, Venevisión, and Televen, have maintained an opposition perspective to Venezuelan politics, some more than others, and the two major national daily newspapers, *El Universal* and *El Nacional,* are undeniably anti-Chávez and anti-revolution, no holds barred. Ninety percent of other print media and radio also continue to be in the opposition camp, while the government and its supporters are left only with state-owned media: Venezolana de Televisión (TV), Vive TV, Radio Nacional de Venezuela, YVKE Mundial, and a rapidly growing network of community-based media with limited reach. Of note is that the Chávez administration has been the major proponent of supporting community and alternative media, providing training, resources, and licenses so local citizen communities can have their voices heard and combat the massive ongoing campaign led by private media that bombards the nation daily with misinformation.

Media outlets such as Globovisión, RCTV, *El Nacional*, and *El Universal* retain close and intimate ties to the State Department through NED and USAID–funded groups such as the Instituto de Prensa y Sociedad (Institute for Press and Society), which regularly hosts "training sessions" and "seminars" for local journalists and communications workers on "reinforcing the capacity of journalists to report on polarized political events in the country."[13] International media associations such as Reporters Without Borders and the Inter-American Press Association (IAPA) have perpetuated the myth that in Venezuela "there is a systematic violation of freedom of expression," yet journalists and media continue to have an unfettered right to disseminate unsubstantiated rumors, harsh and biased criticism of government actions and officials, and completely partisan and anti-Chávez propaganda. In fact, there appears to be an excess of freedom of expression in Venezuela. There are no journalists imprisoned for exercising their rights under the law, nor have any of these media outlets been closed during Chávez's presidency. In reality, the only media and press shut down during the Chávez administration were state media closed by force at the hands of the opposition during the April 2002 coup.[14]

On a national scale in Venezuela, propaganda, media bias, and abuse of constitutional freedoms of expression and press are nothing new. But internationally, the media war has dramatically augmented since early 2005, after the State Department, under Secretary Rice, set the tone in January for an increase in hostilities toward Chávez's government. In fact, right around the time of Condoleezza's confirmation hearing in January 2005, when she made the famous statement regarding Chávez's "negative force" in the region, two of the most renowned U.S. newspapers, the *Washington Post* and the *Wall Street Journal*, published editorials calling for a more "aggressive policy" toward Venezuela due to the "threat" presented by President Chávez in the region. The *Post* editorial also falsely indicated, following the State Department's line, that

Venezuela was starting "an arms race" in the region by purchasing rifles from Russia to replace the forty-year-old rifles used by Venezuela's active armed forces. [15]

That same day, January 14, 2005, the *Washington Times*, a right-wing daily, published declarations from an "anonymous" source in the State Department confirming that the U.S. government was pressuring other nations in Latin America to take a position against the "authoritarian" and "anti-democratic" Chávez administration.[16] And as almost proof of a coordinated campaign between the State Department and the U.S. press, Richard Boucher, spokesman for the Department of State, announced in a press conference that day that "the U.S. government has profound concerns about the anti-democratic and detrimental politics of President Chávez and his government."[17]

These types of comments are not to be taken lightly. By referring to Chávez and his government as "a negative force in the region," "anti-democratic," "authoritarian," and a "threat," the State Department, aided by the U.S. media, is planting the seeds to later justify subsequent actions taken against Venezuela, as was done in the case of Iraq.

Just weeks later, in February 2005, the campaign peaked when Fox News ran a "documentary" titled *The Iron Fist of Hugo Chávez* that painted an image of the Venezuelan leader as "a brutal dictator" providing "refuge to terrorists" and "repressing any opposition" in the nation. Simultaneously, Assistant Secretary of State for Western Hemisphere Affairs Roger Noriega declared on the Voice of America that the "de facto dictator" President Chávez is "threatening the region" and that Washington is actively seeking to "invoke the Democratic Charter" of the Organization of American States to "sanction Venezuela."[18]

Then on February 12, 2005, the front page of the *Miami Herald* headlined, "Chávez Arming to Attack the United States" and featured an article about Venezuela's recent arms purchases from Russia. On page two, the article carried the subtitle "Chávez Arming Venezuela for War with the United States." The use of the word "war" was intentionally misleading and a cause of major alarm. Venezuela at no point has ever indicated intentions to enter into an armed conflict with the United States or any other nation around the world. The *Herald*'s use of semantics was purposefully intended to perpetuate the myth that Chávez was a "serious danger" for the U.S. and actions should be taken against him.

The use of negative terms to describe President Chávez and his government have been inserted into hundreds of press articles in U.S. media and statements made by U.S. officials since early 2005 in a manner that undoubtedly demonstrates a calculated and intentional plan to influence public opinion and perception regarding Venezuela. The obvious purpose is to justify before the international community and the U.S. populace whatever strategy Washington decides to pursue against Chávez and Venezuela.

And the plan has enjoyed relative success.

Take, for example, a commentary in the publication *Parade*, which is distributed to more than 15 million people in the U.S. in the Sunday editions of hundreds of newspapers. The questions and answers section with Walter Scott in the October 9, 2005, edition included the following loaded question:

> I am interested to know where Fidel Castro gets the money to finance his bankrupt regime. Can you explain this to me?

And the answer given by Walter Scott read:

> After the fall of the Soviet Union, which financed Cuba with more than 4 billion dollars annually, Castro found Hugo Chávez, the Marxist president of Venezuela and the fifth largest exporter of oil worldwide. In addition to financing Castro, Chávez is also financing revolutionaries and terrorists throughout Latin America.[19]

So now the average U.S. citizen, sitting at home on a Sunday morning, reading the paper, is informed that President Chávez is funding "terrorists" right next door. No evidence was presented to make such a claim, precisely because none exists, yet the word was out and the seed was planted in the minds of millions of people in the United States that Chávez = Terrorism. Considering the implications of such an equation during times of war, there can be no doubt that the statement was made in order to psychologically prepare average citizens for a conflict with Venezuela. Everyone knows in the United States that under the "War on Terrorism," any nation or leader who relates with terrorists, sponsors them, harbors them or even likes them, is an enemy of the "free world" and will be "taken out." President George W. Bush has said that himself.

It doesn't matter if the information is true—once it's been read or heard, the damage has been done. Nancy Snow wrote about Reagan-era propaganda strategies in her book, *Information War: American Propaganda, Free Speech and Opinion Control Since 9-11*, that appear to parallel the type of tactics in place against Venezuela:

> The pattern was set early in his administration: leak a scare story about foreign enemies, grab the headlines. If, much later, reporters poke holes in the cover story, so what? The truth will receive far less attention than the original lie, and by then another round of falsehoods will be dominating the headlines.[20]

It should be no surprise, then, that the same propaganda makers active during the Reagan administration are today in George W. Bush's government running all the psyops outlets, and they are employing the same methodologies. Since the tactics worked back in the 1980s, there is no reason to believe they won't share similar success today.

As evidence of the success of this psyops strategy against Venezuela to influence perceptions in the U.S. about Chávez and Venezuela, Fox News recently ran a commentary on their website titled "Handling Chávez," stating, "Anti-U.S. leaders Hugo Chávez of Venezuela and Iranian President Mahmoud Ahmadinejad met in Tehran on Saturday, pledging mutual support for one another." The article asked people to respond to the question "If YOU were president, how would you handle Hugo Chávez's overtures to Iran?"[21]

Some of the answers included remarks such as,

> Chávez seems to be arming to spread his "revolution" all across South America. We need to let the citizens of Venezuela know that we totally support their democracy, despite their leader's rhetoric, but we will not

allow any country in South America to be attacked by another Castro wannabe.

—Bill (Albuquerque, NM)

We cannot afford an Iran in our hemisphere. Word needs to get to Chávez that he and his government will be taken down if he aligns his country with Iran, or any other rogue state.

—Ron (Knoxville, TN)

I would sponsor a U.N. resolution stating that Venezuela is a supporter of state-sponsored terrorism.

—Allan

I would make sure that Chávez does not get any aid from the U.S. I would also prohibit travel to Venezuela and triple tax on any U.S. companies that operate there.

—Ray (Mt. Pleasant, MI)

I would immediately put Chávez on the list of terrorists and block imports/exports from his country.

—Cortney

I would not tolerate Chávez. He is a very dangerous man. He may appear harmless, but he is a real threat not only to America but to the entire civilized world!

—Leonard

Hugo Chávez is clearly a threat to humanity and not only to the United States. He is a willing fighter and he is pumping up his military to show it. The U.S. will eventually have to confront him and it would be better sooner than later . . . I would take him out.

—Jerry (Florida)

The above comments were made by people who read and watch Fox News, a right-wing propaganda machine that perpetuates the State Department's myths about Chávez. But the comments show that the propaganda has its effects on the greater population that watches and reads Fox's constant bantering about Venezuela and President Chávez, and they are evidence that the psyops campaign has convinced a sector of the U.S. population that Chávez is a dangerous threat to the United States.

Three Major Lines of Attack

The three major lines of attack in the psyops war against Chávez and Venezuela perpetuate the myths that Chávez is a "dictator," Chávez is "destabilizing and endangering the region, and therefore the national security of the United States" and that Chávez "is a friend of terrorists," which, according to the Bush line of thought, makes Chávez "a terrorist" himself. These falsehoods are regurgitated, recycled, repeated, and reprinted in U.S. and international media over and over again. Just pick up a paper, turn on Fox News, or Google "Chávez" and see for yourself.

The dangerous psyops war against Venezuela is also a war against people around the world. As it intensifies and spreads, the ground will be set on a psychological level to justify "regime change" in Venezuela. The hearts and minds of the people will not just be won over within Venezuela, through its own internal media war and the efforts of special U.S. psyops teams, but also on an international level, where the battlefield has been defined and the "psywarriors" have taken position.

9

Espionage and Sabotage

"Our response will be serious, massive and asymmetric."

—William Brownfield, U.S. ambassador to Venezuela, responding to reporters about how Washington would react to the expulsion of U.S. military attaché Capt. John Correa for espionage activities.

On February 2, 2006, President Hugo Chávez publicly announced the expulsion of a U.S. military attaché, Captain John Correa, accusing him of espionage. Captainn Correa was declared persona non grata and forced to leave Venezuela. He had infiltrated Venezuela's navy and had recruited approximately twenty-five active officers to provide strategic and sensitive information to the Pentagon. Venezuelan military intelligence had detected the irregular activity, penetrated the ring, and denounced the espionage formally to the State Department before expelling Correa, but Washington did not respond.[1] Correa was quietly shuffled out of Venezuela and protected against any legal repercussions through diplomatic immunity.

It is not unusual for the U.S. government to engage in espionage activities in nations around the world. Intelligence gathering and clandestine activities are precisely the duties and objectives of entities such as the Central Intelligence Agency and the Defense Intelligence Agency. However, just because these agencies are charged with espionage missions does not make them legal.

Correa was not the only U.S. spy caught in Venezuela during that year. Other operatives of the Defense Intelligence Agency stationed at the U.S. embassy in Caracas were also discovered infiltrating the Venezuelan armed forces, recruiting "agents" within, and attempting to obtain secret and classified information on internal strategies, plans, and actions. In one particular case, Lieutenant Colonel Humberto Rodriguez, army attaché at the embassy in Caracas and head of its Department of Defense and Operations, was found paying low-ranking Venezuelan soldiers to supply him with strategic information. I had the opportunity to hear classified testimony given in March 2005 by one of the soldiers who had been "recruited" by Lt. Col. Rodriguéz and include a portion of it here. Due to confidentiality, the sections included herein will be limited to information that will not compromise the source.

I am an enlisted soldier pertaining to the action command group. I am testifying about the activities of officials from the United States Embassy (in Caracas). They seek information and analysis about certain activities of members of our Armed Forces. There are members of our military who provide information to Lieutenant Colonel Humberto Rodríguez. He has told me himself that there are officials, I don't know if they are officers or professionals that work with the Minister of Defense, and they give information to him about the activities of the Armed Forces. My job is to try and find certain information and to monitor different political organizations, such as the Tupamaros, Bolivarian Circles, the people who work with Lina Ron, as well as information about the acquisition of arms in the Armed Forces. I note herein that I am working as an infiltrator in these groups, an undercover agent, I do not share the anti-American views of these groups, I am just trying to obtain the best information possible for my superiors, for the defense of our nation.

Q. What do they give you in return?
A. Money, political contacts, and the possibility of work . . .

Q. What is the best they have given you up until now?

A. A ten-year visa to enter the United States, whenever I want, and according to them, in the future I can attend a course in their intelligence agency in the United States once I prove my loyalty to them and they see I truly have guts, I can possibly do an intelligence course with the CIA, that's what the military attaché at the Embassy, Colonel Humberto Rodriguez, told me himself.

Q. When did he tell you that?

A. Approximately one year ago. But they also use different methods of recruitment and they monitor the people that could really work with them and in whom they can trust. So he told me that I am in the process of supervision, in a review process, to see if further along I can opt to study one of those courses, but in reality, my desire is to involve myself more with them to be able to get necessary information that our Department of Military Intelligence needs so it can investigate these people who are coup leaders and traitors to our nation.

Q. Tell me about the last three meetings you have had with them.

A. The last three meetings were in December of last year, one in January and one just this past month in February.

Q. What happened in December of last year?

A. They asked me about the Bolivarian Circles, if they had been given weapons, what kind of training they have. They asked who in the government is managing the reservists, how that whole situation works and they asked me to find out whether or not they were getting weapons, communications equipment and things.

Q. What happened in the meeting in January? What did they say to you in January?

A. He asked me for information about the new arms acquisitions in the Armed Forces, the AK-47 rifles, and he mentioned to me to try and monitor the different "barrios," 23 de Enero, La Vega, and the people who are in charge of the Bolivarian Circles and the groups of reservists. He wanted to know if those weapons were for them. They were interested in knowing if all those weapons were really for the armed forces, or if they were for other groups, the different political organizations, with the intention of strengthening them so they can pressure people during the elections in 2006. Because they believe the arms are to protect the upcoming electoral process, due to the pressure the Americans have put on them. They also asked me to find out about the elections campaign, like who would conform the government's campaign team, what the strategies and plans would be, what projects they have and how the image of Chávez, the comandante, will be projected.

Q. What did they ask you in February?
A. Pretty much what we had talked about before, the Bolivarian Circles, the weapons, the 2006 campaign.

Q. And what did they ask you about the Command Action Group?
A. They asked me about the C4 and if it had been stolen from the Command Action Group, and if the case of C4 had arrived intact. They wanted to know if there were specialists in explosives from the National Guard who were involved in the Danilo Anderson case.

Q. And who do you know of from our military units that are sharing information with them?
A. Yes, I have heard about officers in the ranks of Lieutenant Colonel and Colonel, but I don't know their names, and I know of others that were involved in the coup.

Q. Who?
A. General González González and General Ovidio Pogiolli Perez.

Q. How do you know General Pogiolli was involved with the U.S. military mission?
A. Humberto Rodriguez mentioned him in conversations . . . he said the General was someone not in agreement with President Chávez's politics and way of governing, that he didn't agree with the way he was running the country and that Chávez wasn't prepared to be a president, that he would make a better Minister of Defense, but not a head of state.

Q. What other officers that you know of are giving them information?

A. In the National Guard and the Air Force there are some, but I don't have their exact names.

Q. When you meet with them, do they search you, do they check you thoroughly?
A. No, they ask me if I am carrying a weapon or a cellular phone.

Q. And if you have a cellular phone do they take it from you?
A. They take out the battery and put it in another room. When I talk to them there is always a satellite communications antenna that transmits the information immediately.

Q. What do they give you?
A. About 100,000 bolivares each time.

Q. If you have information for them, how do you contact them?
A. I call him at the U.S. embassy . . . he calls me by a pseudonym and I contact him there on a special number.

One of the most fascinating requests for information that U.S. Army Lieutenant Colonel Humberto Rodriguez makes of the Venezuelan soldier concerns President Chávez's campaign strategies for the 2006 elections and how pro-Chávez social organizations are internally structured. Such information appears outside the realm of military matters, yet Rodriguez's inquiries indicate that the Pentagon is one of the key agencies calculating and preparing strategies and methodologies to be implemented on a "civilian" level in Venezuela. Lt. Col. Rodríguez disappeared from Venezuela soon after Military Intelligence began monitoring his espionage activities.

However, as was the case with Rodríguez and his predecessor, Lieutenant Colonel Bernard Lewis of the U.S. Air Force, who had played the role of spy-runner for the U.S. military mission in Caracas, a replacement would be quick to fill his shoes and continue efforts to obtain strategic and secretive information from internal sources in the Venezuelan government. And with the CIA's new special Mission Manager for Venezuela and Cuba, who heads a special office to increase CIA activities and successes in those nations, the level of espionage and intelligence operations is certain to intensify.

DEA Busted

Drug Enforcement Agency officers working in Venezuela were also exposed during 2005 for sabotaging counter-narcotics missions jointly conducted with Venezuela's National Guard Counter-Narcotics Division and the National Commission Against Illegal Drug Use (CONACUID), and international cooperation agreements to fight drug trafficking were subsequently suspended. This outraged Washington, of course, and swift action was taken to sanction Venezuela in September 2005 for "not cooperating" with counter-narcotics efforts. In reality, it was the other way around.

Brigadier General Frank Morgado, head of the Anti-Drug Command of Venezuela's National Guard, announced publicly in July 2005 that his team would cease collaborations with the DEA based on that agency's lack of cooperation and apparent illegal activity in the country. In March 2005, General Morgado had compiled an extensive dossier documenting unlawful DEA actions that were inhibiting Venezuela's capacity to successfully carry out counter-narcotics missions. In 2002, Venezuela and the U.S. signed agreements that enabled the National Guard and the DEA to collaborate on "special investigations" in the area of drug trafficking. The DEA's involvement in irregular activities in Venezuela dated back to the early 1990s, when confrontations erupted between Venezuelan anti-drug teams and DEA agents over operations and procedures focused on the capture of drug traffickers that appeared to actually facilitate the shipment of considerable volumes of illegal substances to the United States, instead of weakening the drug trade. These incidents resulted in a series of court cases and hearings in Miami and Caracas involving DEA agents and Venezuelan National Guard members, including General Ramon Benigno Guillen Davila, who was the head of the Anti-Drug Command of the National Guard from 1987 to 1991. General Guillen Davila was accused in the federal district court in Florida of drug trafficking based on an allegation made by DEA Inspector Jean Kibble. [2]

In 2005, the DEA-Venezuela conflict came to an all-time high, and General Morgado was able to uncover several specific cases that clearly indicated DEA agent involvement in illegal activity in Venezuela. The intensified DEA sabotage of Venezuelan counter-narcotics efforts was designed to demonstrate that the Venezuelan government was not cooperating on anti-drug trafficking operations and therefore should be sanctioned and classified as a "terrorist" nation. In an internal memo from Venezuela's Financial Intelligence Department, concern was raised about the U.S. government's control over the CONACUID office in Venezuela, which technically is Venezuela's main counter-narcotics agency:

> The government of the United States of America has established a control operations center [in CONACUID], supposedly to support its contributions to the fight against drugs, which to date have been completely inefficient as shown by an increase in drug activities in the nation and more consumption, trafficking and transit, which is causing moral, social and economic damage to Venezuela . . . .These activities developed by the U.S. government have been occurring for a long time and serve as a pretense for the representatives of the United States of America to manipulate results and to try and signal our country as a nation tolerant of drug trafficking and terrorism . . . consequently and with the final intention of inducing the failure of our country to control narcotics traffic . . . .[3]
>
> The penetration and control of the United States of America over the National Commission Against the Illegal Use of Drugs (CONACUID) is evidenced by observing the plans, programs and activities of the agency, which are developed and implemented in concordance with the interests of that country and not developed to favor our nation and government. [4]

General Morgado of the National Guard discovered at minimum three cases of so-called controlled delivery of drug shipments, during which a certain quantity of drugs left Venezuela in the hands of DEA agents, but, once arriving in the United States, the quantities diminished substantially, or in some cases no information whatsoever was given on the receipt of the shipments from the U.S. side. Per an internal memo from the National Guard's Anti-Drug Command:

> The DEA requested on March 16, 2004, through agent Joseph Beckwith, agent in charge of the Office of the DEA in Venezuela at the time, a procedure for a "monitored handover," between March 18 and

April 17, 2004, of fifty (50) kilograms of Cocaine, which were subsequently sent. Once the shipment arrived in the U.S., authorities reported receipt of a shipment consisting of two (02) cardboard boxes that
weighed thirty-five (35) kilograms and resulted in the arrest of individuals in the U.S. and the confiscation of ninety-thousand dollars
($90,000) that was the product of illicit sales. The DEA office in
Caracas never officially notified the Venezuelan authorities as to where
the remaining fifteen (15) kilograms of Cocaine had gone from the original shipment.

Another incident involved the "controlled delivery" of twenty confiscat-
ed kilograms of cocaine on January 20, 2005 to the head of the DEA office
in Caracas, Paul Abosamra, who failed to communicate the results of the
operation to Venezuelan authorities, as specified in the formal cooperation
agreement between the two nations. Another twenty kilograms of cocaine
had just disappeared into the hands of U.S. DEA agents and no formal
inquiries by the U.S. government were ever made, despite repeated requests
from Venezuelan authorities.

In June 2005, two informants in Venezuela publicly denounced the ille-
gal activities of the DEA to Venezuela's attorney general. Venezuela's *El
Nacional* newspaper reported on the incident on July 27, 2005: "A
Venezuelan woman and man sent written reports to the Office of
Fundamental Rights of the Attorney General's office regarding alleged
unlawful operations of the United States Anti-Drug Police in Venezuela. . . .
Two people who claimed to be confidential informants who had been infiltrated into drug trafficking organizations denounced to the Attorney
General's office the alleged illegal activities of DEA agents in Venezuela." In
one of the reports, "the woman revealed to the Prosecutor that she had participated in 'numerous cases where there were apparent irregularities.' The
most important, she added, was the disappearance of 11 kilograms of heroin
during an operation completed in June 2003. She stated she had sent a letter in January 2004 to Washington to denounce the activities of the station
chief of the DEA in Venezuela and the head of the forensic police that
worked with her in the special anti-drug unit. She alleged that the drug confiscation effected on June 14, 2003, contained 21 kilograms of heroin, but

when the laboratory examined the substance to corroborate its composition, it only weighed 10 kilograms."[5]

The Venezuelan government ceased collaborating with the DEA in August 2005, based on numerous detailed reports and evidence of the agency's efforts to sabotage Venezuela's counter-narcotics program. The Bush administration responded with semi-sanctions against Venezuela, stating the South American nation "could no longer be certified as an ally in the war on drugs," and in public statements repeatedly scolded Venezuela for "facilitating" narcotics operations. Venezuela has actually increased its interception and confiscation of illicit drugs in transit through the country and has captured several leading international drug traffickers. The year 2005 was a record year in drug seizures made by the Venezuelan government, with a 58 percent increase from 2004,[6] and in the first trimester of 2006, without DEA "help," the number of drug seizures increased by an additional 30 percent.[7]

Colombian Paramilitaries and Guarimbas

Another major threat facing Venezuela today is the infiltration of thousands of Colombian paramilitaries across Venezuela's borders, many charged with one mission: to assassinate President Chávez. Such a concept may sound ludicrous or fantastical to some, but in Venezuela, it is a threatening reality. In May 2004, more than eighty Colombian paramilitaries were detained in a farm on the outskirts of Caracas belonging to Cuban-Venezuelan Robert Alonso; they were apparently plotting to assassinate President Chávez. Alonso, now self-exiled in Miami, had only months earlier called for widespread civil disobedience and violence throughout the nation in the Guarimba technique, an act intended to provoke repressive reactions by the state that would then justify cries of human rights violations and lack of constitutional order. The Guarimba technique was in fact a concept created with the help of the Albert Einstein Institution (AEI), another U.S. entity funded by the State Department with a very misleading and noble-sounding name.

The AEI is run by Gene Sharp, a self-titled expert of what he calls "non-violent defense," though better termed "regime change." His methodologies have been studied and utilized by opposition movements in Burma, Thailand, Tibet, Belarus, Serbia, Zimbabwe, and Venezuela. In the AEI's 2004 annual report, Venezuela is highlighted as an area where actions are currently being taken:

> Venezuelans opposed to Chávez met with Gene Sharp and other AEI staff to talk about the deteriorating political situation in their country. They also discussed options for opposition groups to further their cause effectively without violence. These visits led to an in-country consultation in April 2003. The nine-day consultation was held by consultants Robert Helvey and Chris Miller in Caracas for members of the Venezuelan democratic opposition. The objective of the consultation was to provide them with the capacity to develop a nonviolent strategy to restore democracy to Venezuela. Participants included members of political parties and unions, nongovernmental organization leaders and unaffiliated activists. . . . Helvey presented a course of instruction on the theory, applications and planning for a strategic nonviolent struggle. Through this, the participants realized the importance of strategic planning to overcome existing shortcomings in the opposition's campaign against Chávez. Ofensiva Ciudadana, a pro-democracy group in Venezuela, requested and organized the workshop. This workshop has led to continued contact with Venezuelans and renewed requests for additional consultations.[8]

How nice of the Albert Einstein Institution to aid Venezuela's opposition in finding new and inventive ways to overthrow Chávez. Robert Helvey, the "consultant" AEI sent to Caracas to help teach the opposition to develop new strategies for regime change in Venezuela, is actually a retired colonel from the U.S. Army, educated at the U.S. Army Command and General Staff College and the U.S. Navy War College.[9] Though Colonel Helvey's bio states he is currently a "strategic planning consultant to non-governmental organizations promoting nonviolent political reforms among pro-democracy movements," in reality he is an expert on low-intensity conflicts, asymmetric war, and regime change. In one of his many public proclamations, Robert Alonso alluded with pride to the fact that he was receiving special "international consulting" for his upcoming plans and strategies to "overthrow the Chávez regime" from Dr. Gene Sharp, "an expert in the matter."

Just months after Colonel Helvey's visit to Caracas, Alonso and his crew began the Guarimbas in February 2004 causing several deaths and injuries and instability throughout the country. Luckily, their "expert" international plan only lasted four days, from February 27 through March 1, 2004, before it was brought to a halt by Venezuelan authorities and citizens who refused to support such atrocious behavior. In a private interview I conducted with an ex-Colombian paramilitary seeking refuge in Venezuela, the role of certain paramilitaries and key Venezuelan opposition extremists in the Guarimba and other acts of violence and destabilization were described.[10] What follows is an extract of that confidential testimony:

> During 2002 I attended the fourth national conference of the United Self-Defense Forces (AUC) and a Venezuelan national of Peruvian descent known as "Pavarotti" was there. He is well known in Venezuela. At the time, I did not know his real name, but now I know his name is Vasco Dakota. It was at the fourth conference of the high level AUC forces where the plans to filter arms across the Venezuelan border from Colombia to use against President Chávez were discussed. And also how to bring over the paramilitaries. The second meeting was held in San Cristobal, Venezuela. Julian Bolívar was there, as well as Vasco Dakota. There was also a Venezuelan National Guard officer there, but I never heard his name. . . . That is when Vasco Dakota stated he would be in charge of the Guarimba.

The ex-Colombian paramilitary also confirmed the large presence of Colombian paramilitaries on Robert Alonso's farm that formed part of a plan to assassinate President Chávez:

> The paramilitaries were infiltrated across the border from Colombia and brought to Caracas and the weapons were supposed to be supplied in Venezuela. But the weapons never appeared. The weapons were sup-

posed to be provided here and there were members of the Venezuelan
military that were working with the paramilitaries. And the purpose of
those paramilitary was to kill President Chávez. They were financed by
the opposition.

He indicated that more than three thousand Colombian paramilitary
were present in the Caracas metropolitan area and thousands more were all
along the Venezuelan-Colombian border. Plans for election year 2006
included the use of explosives, car bombs, and the assassination of members of Venezuela's Congress and other high-level government officials and
public figures. In 2006, there were three assassination attempts against
members of Venezuela's National Assembly, one against Francisco
Ameliach that resulted in the death of his assistant, and two against Braulio
Alvaréz, a land rights activist and congressman for the state of Yaracuy.
Powerful explosives were found in the headquarters of the government's
party, MVR, in the state of Nueva Esparta, and at the doors of the National
Assembly in the nation's capital. There were numerous other incidents of
low-level explosives found in different areas around Caracas and across the
country, including minor explosions in areas around the oil industry.
During the last week of February 2006, Venezuela's DISIP (intelligence
police) discovered 2.2 kilograms of C-4 explosives, ten electric detonators,
and four grenades in the state of Yaracuy. Fortunately, the explosives were
discovered before being used since that quantity could have destroyed a 20-
story building.

Others have been less fortunate. More than 160 farmers and farmer's
rights activists have been killed since 2001 in the rural areas of Venezuela,
many at the hands of paramilitaries hired by large land estate owners refusing to comply with the national Land Reform Law. The U.S. government's
Plan Colombia has been largely responsible for aiding and training paramilitary forces in Colombia to fight against left-wing guerrilla groups that the
U.S. labels "narco-terrorists." The paramilitary forces, who share an ultra-
right-wing ideology, have been viewed as capable of destabilizing
Venezuela's leftist government under the command and control of U.S.
Special Forces stationed in Colombia.

10

Brownfield's Game

William Brownfield seems like such a nice guy. He likes baseball and knows a lot of prominent Major League players whom he enjoys carting all around Venezuela with jolly good old American spirit. He likes jokes and even gets a kick out of pretending he's James Bond, 007, on a great escape mission to flee tomato and egg throwers who can't seem to understand that he means well when he gives giant USAID checks to small community centers and social organizations throughout the country. He scales the mountains of Caracas and climbs the steep barrio steps to reach out wherever he can and spread the goodwill of the United States to the people of Venezuela. He swears his government is not financing any political parties or campaigns in Venezuela, that his embassy "hasn't contributed and won't contribute not one Bolivar, not one cent, to any political party in Venezuela: zero, zero, zero." But as ambassador, he is charged with overseeing the millions in funding USAID is dishing out in Venezuela, including a few hundred thousand annually through the International Republican Institute and the National Democratic Institute, both NED and USAID funded entities, that go toward "strengthening political parties" in the country. The parties involved in those projects include Primero Justicia, Acción Democrática, COPEI, and others aligned with the opposition movement.

Brownfield also likes making public appearances with prominent oppositional presidential candidates, including Manual Rosales, governor of the state of Zulia, and Benjamin Rausseo, a comedian known popularly as "The Count of Guácharo." The ambassador loves to host dinners and receptions with Súmate in his residence and frequently hangs out with key opposition leaders. He would tell you that he doesn't visit frequently with President Chávez or other members of the Venezuelan government because they won't receive him. Poor guy, he tries so hard.

Sometimes, he makes really silly statements to the local press. In June, as the State and Defense Departments ranted and raved about Venezuela's recent arms acquisitions, Ambassador Brownfield declared that "it's Venezuela's sovereign right to buy, sell or build arms" but, he warned, Venezuela has the "obligation" to make such transactions with "transparency."[1] One might ask how possibly more transparent the Venezuelan government could be with its arms purchases. President Chávez consistently announces all such transactions on national television and even hosted an official event with the armed forces where he physically gave soldiers the new Russian rifles that had recently been purchased. And during the military processions on June 24, commemorating the Battle of Carabobo, which was the final battle that led to Venezuela's independence from Spain, and July 5, Independence Day, all the new and old military equipment— including tanks, helicopters and rifles of all types—was openly paraded through the streets and given full media coverage. It would be difficult to get any more transparent.

Brownfield goes where no other U.S. ambassador dares to go: deep into pro-Chávez territory, confident in his mission to bring dollars to the needy. And when his car is pelted with eggs and tropical fruits, he dashes off to the embassy bunker, embedded safe in the Caracas hills. The U.S. State Department rushes to his defense, advising the Venezuelan government that "any incident that could affect the security of embassy personnel, including the Ambassador, raises great concern." Further, the State Department "believes that it is the very important responsibility of a foreign government to collaborate with the embassy of the United States to guarantee that U.S. personnel are protected."[2]

In 1958, during the Venezuela segment of Vice President Richard Nixon's South American tour, he was nearly attacked by angry protesters who demanded he leave the country and the U.S. Marines were sent in to rescue him. "He was met in Venezuela by hostile crowds that spat at him as he left his plane. In the capital, Caracas, the scene turned violent. A mob surrounded his car and began rocking it back and forth, trying to turn it over and chanting 'Death to Nixon.' Protected by only twelve Secret Service agents, the procession was forced to wait for the Venezuelan military to clear a path of escape. But by that time, the car had been nearly demolished and the vice president had seen his fill of South America. President Eisenhower sent a naval squadron to the Venezuelan coast in case they needed to rescue the vice president, but Nixon quietly left the country the next day. He returned to Washington to a hero's welcome."[3]

William Brownfield surely knows that profound piece of U.S. history, as any good and decent functionary of the State Department should. So certainly, when he purposefully goes into pro-Chávez communities and attempts to "win their hearts and minds" with a few thousand dollars, he should know it is provocative. Especially considering that Venezuelans are fully aware of the ongoing activities of USAID and NED in meddling in their internal affairs and financing coup leaders and other destabilizing forces. It would be imprudent to speculate that Brownfield's actions were purposefully seeking violent responses that would endanger him sufficiently to justify a U.S. military rescue mission.

William Brownfield is a career diplomat with senior ranking. He graduated in 1974 from Cornell University, and he subsequently graduated from the National War College in 1993 while a member of the U.S. foreign service. His law school studies were cut short in 1978 and he was sent in 1979 on his first foreign assignment, to Maracaibo, Venezuela, at the height of Venezuela's flourishing and prosperous oil boom. Brownfield has held strategically important and interesting positions in the State Department, ranging from postings in Argentina and El Salvador to Deputy Assistant Secretary of State for Western Hemisphere Affairs, a stint as Director for Policy in the Bureau of International Narcotics and Law Enforcement Affairs, and a brief period as Executive Assistant in the Bureau of Inter-American Affairs. Ambassador Brownfield was also a member of the secretary of state's policy planning staff, and was a special assistant to the Under Secretary for Political Affairs before he became the U.S. ambassador to Chile, the post he held before being assigned to Venezuela in August 2004, during the recall referendum on President Chávez's mandate. One of the more intriguing positions Brownfield held was a special assignment in Panamá as political adviser to the commander-in-chief of the Pentagon's Southern Command during the 1989–90 U.S. invasion of that country.[4]

Brownfield's past experience provides him with substantial expertise in covert operations and U.S. interventions designed to provoke regime change. El Salvador, Argentina, Chile, and Panamá are all nations where the U.S. has invaded or supported coups to topple governments that didn't serve U.S. interests. Brownfield's education at the National War College came after his political advisory function in Panama to none other than the commander in charge of the U.S. invasion. His talents must have been revealed during that mission and he was recommended for further induction into the world of strategic military operations.

In Venezuela, Brownfield came on board at a time when the previous ambassador, Charles Shapiro, had failed on three occasions to achieve U.S. objectives. The miscalculations committed by Shapiro had cost the U.S. government millions of dollars and public shame. Never before in history had a coup effort been so badly bungled as it was in April 2002 in Venezuela. Brownfield was sent in to clean up Shapiro's mess. As a dedicated professional, he has done quite well. The dollars flooding into opposition groups have increased and expanded in reach and Venezuela has inched closer and closer to a stigmatized position in the international community among U.S. allies. The range of covert and overt operations of the U.S. embassy and its affiliates in Caracas have spread throughout the nation, successfully seeking creative outlets to conduct missions and meet objectives without prior detection.

Since November 2004, Ambassador Brownfield has made more than thirty-five public visits to different states and cities throughout Venezuela, donating USAID funds to distinct local Venezuelan entities. He has attempted to project the "friendly face" of the U.S. in poor communities, playing the "good cop, bad cop" role. He's the good cop, and all the rest of the U.S. officials up in Washington are the "bad cops," constantly lashing out at Venezuela and President Chávez with an aggressive discourse. He has been successful in his efforts to spread U.S. funding into the depths of Venezuela's poorer communities, many of which are majority Chávez supporters. He has also helped to build relationships between opposition municipal mayors in Caracas, such as Leopoldo Lopez of Chacao and Henrique Capriles Radonsky of Baruta, and the Federal Bureau of Investigation. Brownfield set up several exchange and training programs in early 2005 between the FBI and the Chacao and Baruta local police forces, bypassing the national government. It seems as though an arrangement between a foreign intelligence service and a municipal government should have authorization from the Foreign Ministry and the Ministry of the Interior, which is in charge of intelligence activities. But in the typical arrogant style of the United States, Ambassador Brownfield just went ahead and facilitated the "exchange" with the FBI without notifying the Venezuelan government.[5]

American Corners

One of the recent initiatives Brownfield has implemented in Venezuela are the American Corners. The Corners are officially partnership programs between the U.S. embassy and local institutions that create small spaces—corners—where access is provided to information about the United States through the internet and through books and documentaries produced by the State Department. The idea is to create a type of "satellite consulate" not formally hosted by the U.S. government but rather by a local organization, association, school, library or institution. American Corners serves as yet another propaganda tool of the U.S. government that not only functions as a launching point of the psyop war but also subverts and violates diplomatic regulations by placing small "consular" access sites in a nation without authorization from the host government. The Corners are closely monitored by the State Department, which keeps tabs on their effectiveness.

The American Corners concept was created in the 1990s and first inaugurated by the U.S. government in Russia. The idea was to preserve the advances and work that had been done during the Cold War and to continue a low-profile presence to assure U.S. propaganda and information was still effective. In 2002, the American Corners program was expanded by the Office for Public Diplomacy and Public Affairs of the U.S. State Department, and today more than two hundred Corners exist around the world. The majority of the American Corners were placed in Eastern European nations, such as Bulgaria, Poland, Uzbekistan, Kyrgyzstan, and Turkey; Asian nations, such as Pakistan, Indonesia, and Bangladesh; and countries in the Middle East, including Afghanistan and Oman, among others.[6] Venezuela is the first nation in Latin America to be a part of the American Corners program.

In 2006, Ambassador William Brownfield inaugurated four American Corners in Venezuela, in the cities of Barquisimeto, Margarita, Maturín, and Lecherías, in the state of Anzoátegui. The Corners in Barquisimeto, Margarita, and Maturín are all hosted by regional lawyers' associations, including the Colegio de Abogados (Lawyers' Association) in the state of Lara, which also receives financing from the National Endowment for Democracy. In the case of Lecherías, in the state of Anzoátegui, the Corner is placed in the offices of the municipal government, which is run by an opposition mayor. According to the U.S. embassy in Venezuela, "The function of the American Corner is Lecherías is to be the center for study and information. The Corner offers books written by a great variety of American authors and free internet access for local individuals interested in learning. It provides current news about the United States and it also hosts events and activities that feature American culture. The fundamental task of the American Corner is to provide the general public with access to information on the United States of America." [7]

Sound harmless?

The "fundamental task" of the American Corner is clearly a function of the diplomatic representatives of the United States and not of local governments or local institutions. It is perfectly acceptable within international diplomacy law for a government to promote itself within a foreign nation where it has diplomatic representation. But the Corners go beyond this notion by passing off diplomatic activities to local entities and covertly inserting U.S. propaganda into communities through so-called information centers. The State Department's Office of Public Diplomacy and Public Affairs, overseen by then-Under Secretary Karen Hughes, a close advisor to President George W. Bush since his years as the governor of Texas, had a more than $600 million annual budget allotted to propaganda and information activities to change perceptions about the United States worldwide. The Office of

Public Diplomacy was formally incorporated in an attempt to continue the functions of the U.S. Information Agency (USIA), the previous propaganda branch of the U.S. government that was merged into the State Department in 1999. The American Corners serve as a fundamental part of the new "public diplomacy" effort in nations where popular perceptions about the United States are negative. A branch of the Corners can be launched with a minimal investment of $25,000, for example, and inserted into local communities to function as spot-based propaganda units on a regional level.

In Venezuela, Ambassador Brownfield slipped four American Corners into locations across the nation without advising the Venezuelan government of his diplomatic outreach efforts. Clearly, attempts to shade and cloak the new "satellite consulates" indicate not only their subversive intentions but also their illegality.

Electoral Intervention

During a 2005 visit to Maracaibo, in the state of Zulia, Ambassador William Brownfield proclaimed to the local press, "Twenty-five years ago I lived in the Independent Western Republic of Zulia, so I know what heat is."[8] Yes, Zulia has a hot climate, and not just because of its warm weather. Zulia's national security interests, insecure border with Colombia, major developed oil industry, opposition governor turned presidential candidate, and recent separatist movement have made it a point of contention and concern for the people of Venezuela. Brownfield frequently travels to Zulia and is known to be a close friend of the state's governor, Manuel Rosales. He is a supporter of autonomous stature for Zulia and runs an ongoing campaign using slogans such as "Zulia First" and "Zulia On Its Own Path," and is openly opposed to the national government run by President Chávez.

The idea of separatism in Zulia became public during 2005, as more and more propaganda, advertisements, and declarations were made regarding such desires within the state. The organization Rumbo Propio, or "Our Own Path," began a publicity campaign with billboards and advertisements promoting the concept of separatism with slogans such as "Liberal Capitalism, the hope of the people."

In early 2006, on the "Day of Zulia," Ambassador Brownfield was invited as a special guest to the events and appeared on a local television program. He indicated that "Zulia is the best state in Venezuela" and that he
"enjoyed" being there. A subsequent proposal released by Rumbo Propio
proclaimed the necessity for a "Statute of Zulia" that would be based on the
Venezuelan constitution of 1961, which no longer holds legal validity but
indicates the group's clear anti-democratic intentions. The group has called
for a plebiscite to create the statute, which would declare Zulia an
autonomous state with its own form of neoliberal capitalist government.[9]

The issue of autonomy or separatism in Zulia relates to the candidacy of
Manuel Rosales as president of the nation. The opposition's ongoing campaign to question the legitimacy of the National Elections Council, which
oversees all electoral processes in the country, made for speculation as to
whether the opposition and Rosales would accept the outcome of the
December 2006 presidential elections. While Rosales and his supporters
did attempt to claim the elections were fraudulent, which Chávez won with
a landslide 64 percent of the vote, they eventually accepted the results,
promising to continue their "fight" from "the streets." If they had refused to
recognize the legality of the elections and their outcome, it could have
opened the doors for Rosales to proclaim Zulia as an independent state that
would not recognize the new Chávez administration.

The fact that Zulia is the region where the developed oil industry is
located and has already, with Plan Balboa, been the subject of an "invasion
plan," makes such a possibility more real. There is no question that the
presence of William Brownfield in Venezuela aided in the increase in hostil-
ity and aggression of the U.S. government toward President Chávez and his
administration. During Brownfield's reign, propaganda campaigns substantially increased and U.S. government programs, plans, and agents penetrated Venezuelan society to a dangerous level.

In the summer of 2007, William Brownfield was named U.S. ambassador to Colombia, and Patrick Duddy, former Assistant Sub-Secretary of
State for the Southern Cone, Brazil, and the Caribbean, became the new
ambassador to Venezuela. Duddy's assignment to Venezuela makes him the
highest-level official in the State Department to serve as ambassador in
Latin America, which emphasizes the level of priority the United States is

now placing on Venezuela. Duddy holds a Master's Degree in National Security Strategy from the National War College in the United States. He previously held posts in Bolivia and Brazil, and is certain to use that experience and knowledge to increase efforts to block the region's move toward integration and independence from the United States and international financial institutions. Brownfield will continue to collaborate with Duddy from neighboring Colombia, and relations between Venezuela and the United States are certain to deteriorate as the United States steps up its aggression toward the Venezuelan government.

11

Conclusion

In March 2006, agents of the FBI's counter-terrorism task force in southern California interrogated Pomona College professor Miguel Tinker-Salas in his university office, questioning him about the Venezuelan community in the Los Angeles area, indicating they were suspected of terrorism. The FBI agents also asked Professor Tinker-Salas about his relationship to the Venezuelan government, if any, and whether or not he had been asked to speak favorably about the Chávez administration. Though it was a "fishing expedition," as Tinker-Salas, a Venezuelan-American history professor, later proclaimed, the incident was intended to intimidate and silence those who criticize the Bush government's policy toward Venezuela. The FBI agents also questioned college students in the hallway outside the professor's office, in clear violation of their rights, and took down notes about the postings on Tinker-Salas's office door.[1]

The Tinker-Salas interrogation was the first public occurrence involving U.S. law enforcement harassment of Chávez supporters in the United States. Interestingly, and alarmingly, Professor Tinker-Salas is not a political activist. He is a professor of Latin American history at Pomona College and a known expert on U.S. foreign policy in Latin America, particularly Venezuela and Mexico. Yet he was singled out by the FBI and chosen to be the first case of persecution for politically supporting the politics of the Venezuelan government. No other university professors are known to have received similar harassment to date.

Thought police? McCarthyism? Does this imply that freedom of thought and expression are no longer protected in any arena in the United States, including the sacred academic sphere? It is possible, as the Bush administration encroaches more and more on the basic rights guaranteed in the U.S. Constitution in the name of the war on terror, that those who show a favorable opinion of the Venezuelan government or its people will be considered suspect. Logically, if the U.S. government is waging a psychological and asymmetrical war against Venezuela, it will have repercussions for people within the United States who support Chávez or are interested in finding out more about the Bolivarian revolution.

Ironically, while the U.S. government considers pro-Chávez activists a potential "terrorist threat" to the nation, the Bush administration has gone overboard to provide refuge to one of Latin America's most notorious terrorists, Luis Posada Carriles, responsible for more than a hundred bombing attempts and the explosion of the Cuban airliner in 1976 that killed all 73 passengers aboard. Posada Carriles illegally entered the United States in March 2005 and requested political asylum. Venezuela filed for extradition, since Posada holds both Cuban and Venezuelan nationality and is a fugitive from justice in Venezuela. He escaped from a Venezuelan prison after being arrested for the plane bombing and fled the country over twenty years ago. The U.S. has refused to grant the extradition request that would return Posada Carriles to Venezuela, citing a possible risk that he would be "tortured" were he released to Venezuelan authorities. The U.S. presented no reliable evidence to demonstrate this allegation, preferring to give liberty to a terrorist.

Are the people of the United States willing to let their government take the conflict with Venezuela a step further in their name? It wouldn't be the first time.

This book has outlined the current strategies and methodologies the U.S. government is employing against Venezuela to undermine its democracy, sabotage its economy and society, and overthrow its democratically elected and popularly supported leader. These active tactics and plans are being implemented as tools of aggression against a peaceful people seeking to create a social and political system that is inclusive and beneficial to all their citizens. As you read these words, the Pentagon, State Department, and CIA are devising new lines of attack to achieve their goals in Venezuela and are harming the lives of innocent, humble Venezuelans.

What has Venezuela done to the United States to deserve such treatment?

In September 2005, the Venezuelan government donated $1 million in oil, food, and equipment to the victims of Hurricane Katrina, channeled through its U.S.-based, but Venezuelan-owned, Citgo Petroleum Corporation.

The Bush administration didn't like that, especially because Venezuela almost responded quicker than the U.S. officials who, in any event, failed to effectively aid the primarily poor, minority victims of the Katrina tragedy.

In late 2005, the Venezuelan government, through its Citgo Petroleum Corporation, began a program to offer discounted heating oil to low-income residents in the United States in an effort to continue its policy of non-exploitation of poor people. President Chávez had first launched this concept of helping out poorer people in the United States during a trip to the Bronx a few months earlier, when he was struck by the level of poverty that existed in the richest nation in the world. Citgo, owned by Venezuela's state oil company, Petróleos de Venezuela, S.A. (PDVSA), has seven refineries and over 14,000 gas stations in the United States and generates millions in profits. Chávez decided that he would apply the same policies he implements in Venezuela through PDVSA in the United States: helping the poor to meet basic needs and rise out of poverty.

Initially, the program was to be activated in Boston and New York, but it received such an outstanding reaction that more than six other cities and communities were added. The programs are run through Citgo and local nonprofit organizations that act as coordinators for communities to receive the discounted heating oil. The first phase of the program was in Boston and it involved up to 12 million gallons of heating oil with discounts from market prices. The value of these discounts was nearly $10 million at current market prices. Other cases include:

- In New York, Citgo is providing up to 8 million gallons of discounted heating oil, which will result in millions of dollars in savings.

- In Maine, Citgo provided 8 million gallons of heating oil at a 40 percent discount to low-income families. This aid also assisted homeless shelters and four Native American tribes.

- In Rhode Island, Citgo provided 3.3 million gallons of discounted home heating oil to low-income families, homeless shelters, and community clinics.

- In Pennsylvania, Citgo provided 5 million gallons of heating oil at a 40 percent discount that benefited as many as 25,000 low-income families in the Philadelphia region.

- In Vermont, Citgo provided 2.4 million gallons of Venezuelan oil to low-income Vermonters at a 40 percent discount, with an additional 108,000 gallons donated to homeless shelters for free.

- In Delaware, Citgo distributed 1 million gallons of heating oil to low-income residents at a 40 percent discount, which benefited about 5,000 low-income households in Delaware. Twenty homeless shelters received 150,000 gallons of free heating fuel.

- In Connecticut, Citgo assisted in providing 4.8 million gallons of discounted heating oil to low-income consumers and 54,000 gallons of no-cost heating oil to homeless shelters.[2]

The Bush administration doesn't like the program. It claims that Chávez is attempting to "buy" political support in the United States through offering reduced-cost heating oil to low-income communities. The Bush administration cannot comprehend why any oil company would give discounts to buyers, no matter how poor they are, unless it has a hidden agenda. Citgo is in fact the only oil company in the U.S. that has created and implemented such a socially conscious program. Citgo actually does not generate any losses from the discounts, which basically just cut out the middle-man and supplies the heating oil directly to communities using local nonprofits as facilitators. Through the Citgo discounted heating oil program, the Chávez administration is showing consistency and solidarity with its policies, not just preserving beneficial social programs for its own people but also for those nations around the world where it has shared long-term partnerships and relationships.

What else doesn't the Bush administration like about Venezuela?

It doesn't like the fact that through investing its own oil profits from PDVSA into domestic social programs, millions of medical cases have been attended to under Mission Barrio Adentro, which provides free medical services to Venezuelans with the generous support of Cuban doctors stationed in Venezuela. It doesn't like Mission Robinson, which has successfully eradicated illiteracy in Venezuela in less than two years and taught more than two million Venezuelans to read and write, free of cost. It certainly doesn't approve of Mission Ribas and Mission Sucre, that provide access to continuing secondary education and higher education programs for all Venezuelans, also for free. Mission Habitat, which is building free housing for tens of thousands of Venezuelans across the nation, does not meet Washington's approval, nor does Mission Milagro, which has provided free eye surgeries for more than 12,500 patients in Venezuela, Bolivia, Ecuador, Jamaica, and even the United States. Mission Vuelvan Caras, which provides job training and technical skills knowledge to citizens free of charge, is also frowned upon by the U.S. government.

Why?

Because these successful social programs prove that a government can invest in its people without compromising the economy. Venezuela's social model has shown that it is actually more prosperous for a government to ensure its citizens are well educated, healthy, and have the skills needed to enter the workforce, and that such an ambitious concept is possible, even in today's world of globalization.

The U.S. government doesn't like this model, because it exposes its own inefficiencies, its disregard for its citizens, and its exploitative and selfish model that actually increases poverty and depression throughout the nation. Venezuela offers an alternative—a successful, prosperous, and humane alternative that threatens U.S. domination in the world because it is a model that other nations have already begun to build on. The face of Latin America is rapidly changing. More socially oriented governments are being elected throughout the region in Bolivia, Argentina, Brazil, Uruguay, and Chile, and others are likely to move in the same direction.

Washington's war against Venezuela will continue to increase as it loses its grip on power in the region. Remember, Venezuela is the nation with the

largest oil reserves in the world. Venezuela's Faja Orinoco River basin has
more than 300 billion barrels of petroleum and other parts of the nation are
rich in minerals, natural gas, and coal. The United States model of excessive
consumption is dependent upon these resources, and though Venezuela has
not threatened to deprive the American people of these resources, looking
north is no longer Venezuela's priority.

This book has presented some of the ways U.S. aggression manifests
itself, though other methods will surely surface as new developments occur.
The people of the United States have the choice of supporting
Washington's unjust and dangerous war against a peaceful nation or actively taking the initiative to halt any further efforts to violate Venezuela's sovereign right to self-determination. People around the world are already rising
up against such aggressions and defending their rights against U.S. domination and bullying tactics.

The U.S. Declaration of Independence endows citizens with the power
to stop their government from violating their rights to "life, liberty and the
pursuit of happiness." Those rights are violated every day in the United
States, and in nations such as Afghanistan, Cuba, Iraq, and Venezuela at the
hands of the Bush administration.

> Whenever any Form of government becomes destructive of these ends, it
> is the Right of the People to alter or to abolish it, and to institute new
> government, laying its foundation on such principles and organizing its
> power in such form, as to them shall seem most likely to effect their
> Safety and Happiness.[3]

It is time to invoke that power and implement that right. Otherwise, the
global war waged by U.S. imperialism will never end.

Notes

Introduction

1. The Carmona swearing-in ceremony was broadcast live on all private television channels in Venezuela. The document signed by those present was later left in the Presidential Palace after the coupsters were forced out. On September 19, 2004, government prosecutor Danilo Anderson announced he would begin to issue subpoenas to all 395 signers of the document. See http://www.monthlyreview.org/bushvchavez.htm, Appendix 3, for documentary evidence of a U.S. military role in the coup.

2. On the morning of April 12, 2002, White House spokesperson Ari Fleischer stated: "We know that the action encouraged by the Chávez government provoked this crisis. According to the best information available, the Chávez government suppressed peaceful demonstrations. Government supporters, on orders from the Chávez government, fired on unarmed, peaceful protestors, resulting in 10 killed and 100 wounded. The Venezuelan military and the police refused to fire on the peaceful demonstrators and refused to support the government's role in such human rights violations. The government also tried to prevent independent news media from reporting on these events. The results of these events are now that President Chávez has resigned the presidency. Before resigning, he dismissed the vice president and the cabinet, and a transitional civilian government has been installed." Available at http://www.whitehouse.gov/news/releases/2002/04/20020412-1.html.

3. Cable sent from the U.S. eembassy in Caracas by Ambassador Charles Shapiro, obtained under the Freedom of Information Act by Eva Golinger and Jeremy Bigwood. Available at http://www.venezuelafoia.info.

4. On Sunday, April 14, 2004, on NBC News' *Meet the Press,* Condoleeza Rice stated: "Well, I hope that Hugo Chávez takes the message that his people sent him that his own policies are not working for the Venezuelan people, that he's dealt with them in a high-handed fashion. And I hope what he said in his speech this morning, that he understands that this is a time for national reflection, that he recognizes it's time for him to reflect on how Venezuela got to where it is. He needs to respect constitutional processes. This is no time for a witch hunt. This is time for national reconciliation in Venezuela. And we are working with our partners in the OAS and in the region to try and help Venezuela through this very difficult time. But we do hope that Chávez

recognizes that the whole world is watching, and that he takes advantage of this opportunity to right his own ship, which has been moving, frankly, in the wrong direction for quite a long time."

5. See "National Endowment for Democracy: A Foreign Policy Branch Gone Awry," a Policy Report by the Council on Hemispheric Affairs and the Inter-Hemispheric Education Resource Center, 1990. Today, Republican Senator John McCain and Democrat, former secretary of state, Madeline Albright oversee the International Republican Institute and National Democratic Institute, respectively.

6. See William Robinson, *A Faustian Bargain: U.S. Intervention in the Nicaraguan Elections and American Foreign Policy in the Post-Cold War Era* (Boulder: Westview Press, 1992), 93. Beatríz Rángel currently works with the Cisneros Group of Companies in New York and Miami, the multinational corporation owned by media mogul Gustavo Cisneros, a Cuban-Venezuelan alledgedly involved in the April 2002 coup. Until mid-2004, Rángel was also a board member of the Inter-American Dialogue, a Washington think tank highly critical of the Chávez administration.

7. The CTV continues to be one of NED's major recipients in Venezuela, as well as a clear instrument of U.S. policy, evident through the union's key role in the 2002 coup and the subsequent illegal oil industry strike in winter 2002–03.

8. See William Blum, *Killing Hope: U.S. Military and C.I.A. Interventions Since World War II* (Monroe, Maine: Common Courage Press, 2004), 163–72.

9. See Eva Golinger, *The Chávez Code: Cracking US Intervention in Venezuela* (Northampton, Mass.: Olive Branch Press, 2006), Chapter 8.

10. See Eva Golinger, *The Chávez Code*, Chapter 8.

11. There are hundreds of complaints filed with the Inter-American Commission on Human Rights that appear to be without merit. There have also been complaints filed against the Chávez government in the International Criminal Court in The Hague and in the Southern District Court in Miami alleging human rights abuses. There has been no decision made in either of these courts on whether the cases should be allowed to proceed.

12. See Linda Robinson, "Terror Close to Home," *U.S. News and World Report*, October 2003. Robinson attempts to link al-Qaeda, FARC, and ELN terrorists to the Chávez government.

13. Cable declassified by our FOIA requests. See: http://www.venezuelafoia.info.

14. On February 13, 2002, Carlos Ortega met with Otto Reich in Washington. See http://www.state.gov/r/pa/prs/dpb/2002/8034.htm.

15. See David Corn, "Our Gang in Venezuela?," *The Nation*, August 5, 2002.

16. See http://www.venezuelafoia.info/NED/IRI/2001-047QR-Oct-Dec/pages/2001-047QR-Oct-Dec-04.htm and http://www.venezuelafoia.info/NED/ACLV/2003-545/pages/ACLV-metroRepre-01.htm.

17. Cable from the U.S. embassy to Washington, April 11–12, 2002. Available at http://www.venezuelafoia.info.

18. Taken from USAID's background description of its OTI in a $10 million contract between USAID and Development Alternatives Inc. for projects in Venezuela during August 2002–August 2004.

19. Ibid.

20. See Joel M. Jutkowitz, "Building Confidence Out of Discord in Venezuela," DAI News, http://www.dai.com/dai_news/text_only/fall_confidence_in_venezuela_text_only.htm

21. DAI grant, G-3822-101-008, available at http://www.venezuelafoia.info. Please note that USAID and DAI deleted the names of all recipients of the Venezuela project funds. Their stated reason was "fear of persecution" from the Venezuelan government for the groups they were financing.

22. See http://colombia.indymedia.org/news/2004/05/12839.php.

23. Cable from the U.S. embassy in Caracas, August 14, 2002. Available at http://www.venezuelafoia.info.

24. See http://www.whitehouse.gov/news/releases/2002/12/20021213.html.

25. See http://www.state.gov/r/pa/prs/dpb/2002/15976.htm.

26. Department of Defense cable available at http://www.venezuelafoia.info.

27. SAIC had recently taken over the development of security systems and databases for electronic voting machines in the U.S. market.

28. See http://www.venezuelafoia.info/USAID/USAID-index.htm and http://www.venezuelafoia.info/NED/SUMATE/SUMATE%20index.htm.

29. See http://www.sumate.org.

30. Department of Defense report available at http://www.venezuelafoia.info.

31. See http://www.venezuelafoia.info/NED/CIPE-CEDICE/CEDICE-index.htm.

32. See http://www.venezuelafoia.info/NED/Memorandum/pages/Memorandum-D40.htm.

33. On Friday, August 20, 2004, Roger Noriega, Assistant Secretary for Western Hemisphere Affairs of the State Department, stated, "We have invested a lot of money in the democratic process because we have faith in civil society, which is a pillar of representative democracy. We have given money to similar types of NGOs in Venezuela by means of the State Department and USAID. Civic groups with the mission to defend their democratic institutions and demand basic rights for Venezuelans also represent a good investment."

34. See "U.S. firm embroiled in Venezuela referendum controversy defends its exit poll," Associated Press, August 19, 2004; available at http://www.sfgate.com/cgi-bin/article.cgi?file=/news/archive/2004/08/19/international2018EDT0734.DTL&type=printable.

35. "Violence will allow us to remove him. That's the only way we have... [Chávez] must die like a dog, because he deserves it." Ex-President Carlos Andres Perez, interview in El Nacional, July 26, 2004. See also, http://perso.wanadoo.es/camilofidel/2004/JULIO/26-07-04carlos-andres-perez.htm.

1. Washington's Ongoing War on Venezuela: An Overview

1. Nestor Ikeda, "Bush requests diverse aid for the region, including Venezuela," Miami Herald, Feb. 7, 2005.

2. See http://www.amcornersvenezuela.org/main.php.

3. See http://embajadausa.org.ve/wwwh2761.html.

4. See http://www.whitehouse.gov/news/releases/2005/09/20050915-1.html.

5. Statement on President Authorizing Secretary of State to Transmit to Congress Annual Report Listing Major Illicit Drug-Producing and Drug-Transit Countries, September 15, 2005, http://www.whitehouse.gov/news/releases/2005/09/20050915-1.html.

6. H. CON. RES. 400, "Urge Venezuela to Help Combat Narco-Trafficking in our Hemisphere," available at http://www.house.gov/international_relations/.

7. Cable sent from the U.S. embassy in Caracas to the State Department, January 2005. See http://www.monthlyreview.org/bushvchavez.htm, Appendix 1, A1.1.

8. See http://news.bbc.co.uk/2/hi/americas/4723902.stm.

9. Ibid.

10. Doctrine for Joint Psychological Operations, Department of Defense, available at http://www.gwu.edu/~nsarchiv/NSAEBB/ NSAEBB177/02_psyop-jp-3-53.pdf and www.iwar.org.uk/psyops/resources/us/jp3_53.pdf.

2. Condi Rice's Negative Force

1. "Rice: Venezuela's Chávez 'Negative Force' in the Region," *Wall Street Journal*, January 18, 2005.

2. Testimony of Director of Central Intelligence Porter J. Goss Before the Senate Select Committee on Intelligence, 16 February 2005. Available at http://www.cia.gov.

3. "A Year Later, Goss's CIA Is Still in Turmoil," *Washington Post*, October 19, 2005.

4. "Goss Plans to Expand CIA Spying and Analysis," *Washington Post*, September 23, 2005.

5. See http://www.dni.gov/press_releases/News_Release_16_08_18_06.pdf.

6. See http://www.monthlyreview.org/bushvchavez.htm, Appendix 1, A1.2, A1.3.

7. Assistant Secretary Noriega's Statement before the Senate Foreign Relations Committee, March 2, 2005. Available at http://www.state.gov.

8. "What to Do About Venezuela," Center for Security Policy, May 2005. Available at http://www.centerforsecuritypolicy.org.

9. The Project for a New American Century (PNAC) is a think tank created by neoconservatives that has laid out the strategy for dominating energy reserves in the Middle East. PNAC promotes a "neo-Reaganite" foreign policy based on "military force and moral clarity." In September 2000, PNAC released a report titled "Rebuilding America's Defenses: Strategy, Forces and Resources for a New Century." Since 1998, PNAC had called for the unilateral removal of Saddam Hussein from power in Iraq and immediately after the attacks on September 11, 2001, PNAC published a letter calling for a declaration of "Global War Against Terrorism." PNAC's Board of Directors and related friends includes characters such as Donald Rumsfeld, Elliot

Abrams, Jeb Bush, Paula Dobriansky, Francis Fukuyama, Frank Gaffney, Vin Weber (NED), John Bolton, Robert Zoellick, Morton Abramaowitz, Frank Carlucci, and others.

10. "What to Do About Venezuela," 1.

11. "What to Do About Venezuela," 2.

12. Constitution of the Bolivarian Republic of Venezuela, 1999.

13. "What to Do About Venezuela," 3.

14. See Eva Golinger, *The Chávez Code: Cracking US Intervention in Venezuela* (Northampton, Mass.: Olive Branch Press, 2006), 119–23.

15. "What to Do About Venezuela," 7–11.

16. "What to Do About Venezuela," 12.

17. Ibid.

18. "What to Do About Venezuela," 13–14.

19. "What to Do About Venezuela," 14.

20. See http://www.centerforsecuritypolicy.org.

21. See http://en.wikinews.org/wiki/US_Secretary_of_Defense_Donald_Rumsfeld_visits _Brazil.

22. Donald Rumsfeld, interview with Andrés Oppenheimer, April 5, 2005, http://ciponline.org/facts/050405rums.htm.

23. "Rumsfeld Questions Possible Venezuela-Russia Arms Deal," Voice of America, March 23, 2005, http://www.voanews.com/english/archive/2005-03/2005-03-23-voa82. cfm?CFID=42820299&CFTOKEN=40071679.

24. "Pardo-Maurer Speaks at the Hudson Institute's Center for Latin American Studies," U.S. Cuba Policy Report, July 26, 2005, Special Edition.

25. Ibid.

26. "Roundtable Interview with the President and Foreign Media," Roosevelt Room, White House, May 5, 2005.

27. See http://www.rethinkvenezuela.com/downloads/milspend.htm.

28. Heritage Foundation, "U.S. Policy Toward Latin America: A Legacy of Uneven Engagement," August 23, 2005.

29. "Fiscal Year 2006 National Defense Authorization Budget Request," testimony of General Bantz J. Craddock, Commander, U.S. Southern Command, hearing of the House Armed Services Committee, March 9, 2005; available at http:// ciponline.org/ colombia/050309crad.htm.

30. House Representative Connie Mack (FL), speech before the House on July 14, 2005.

31. See Golinger, *The Chávez Code*, 94–101.

32. "Robertson Called for the Assassination of Venezuela's President," August 22, 2005, http://mediamatters.org/items/200508220006.

33. "Robertson Again Calls for Chávez's Assassination: Not Now, but One Day," February 3, 2006, http://mediamatters.org/items/200602030003.

34. See http://en.wikipedia.org/wiki/Monroe_Doctrine.

35. Statement by John Negroponte to the Senate Select Committee on Intelligence, February 2, 2006.

36. MSNBC, "Rumsfeld Likens Venezuela's Chávez to Hitler Defense, Chief Expresses Concern at 'Populist Leadership' in Latin America," February 3, 2006, http://www.msnbc.msn.com/id/11159503/.

37. National Security Strategy of the United States of America, March 16, 2006. http://www.whitehouse.gov/nsc/nss/2006/index.html.

38. "Bush: Choose Democracy," November 7, 2005, http://www.cbsnews.com/stories/2005/11/04/world/main1009964.shtml.

39. U.S. State Department, *2005 Report on Terrorism*.

40. "Venezuela and Terrorists," *Washington Times*, May 21, 2006.

41. "US General James T. Hill Admits No Evidence to Link Venezuela with Colombian Guerrillas," October 21, 2003, http://www.vheadline.com/readnews.asp?id=12023.

42. "Bush Manifests His Concern for Venezuela," *El Universal*, June 7, 2006.

43. See http://www.state.gov/s/ct/rls/crt/2006/82735.htm.

3. The Money Pot Grows:
The National Endowment for Democracy

1. "Bush Requests Diverse Aid for the Region, Including Venezuela," *Miami Herald*, February 7, 2006.

2. Eva Golinger, *The Chávez Code: Cracking US Intervention in Venezuela* (Northampton, Mass.: Olive Branch Press, 2006), 16–24, but I sincerely recommend you read the entire book to understand fully the extent of NED operations in Venezuela.

3. "Ethiopia Expels US-funded Pro-Democracy Groups Ahead of Elections," March 31, 2005, http://reliefweb.int/rw/rwb.nsf/f303799b16d2074285256830007fb33f/62aab4af111fa0b1c1256fd50047ad 2a?OpenDocument.

4. Cable from the U.S. embassy in Caracas to the Department of State, authored by Ambassador William Brownfield. Obtained under the Freedom of Information Act and available in the author's files.

5. "NGOs a Cover for Spying in Russia," *Moscow Times*, May 13, 2005, http://www.globalresearch.ca/index.php?context= viewArticle&code=20050513&articleId=139.

6. Anthony Fenton and Dennis Bernstein, "AP Reporter Regine Is Wearing Two Hats," *Flashpoints*, December 30, 2005; http://www.haitiaction.net/News/FP/12_29_5/12_29_5.html.

7. The four core groups of NED, the International Republican Institute (IRI), National Democratic Institute (NDI), Center for International Private Enterprise (CIPE), and American Center for International Labor Solidarity (ACILS), were created to filter funding to political parties, labor unions, and business associations in order to

bypass congressional regulations that NED could not directly finance political parties and campaigns. See Golinger, *Chávez Code*, 16–17.

8. Joshua Kurlantzick, "The Coup Connection," *Mother Jones*, November/December 2004, available at http://www.motherjones.com/news/outfront/2004/11/11_401.html.

9. See USAID Budget Request, http://www.usaid.gov/policy/budget/cbj2007/summtabs/st_7.pdf.

10. See how Venezuela is conveniently excluded from the list at http://www.usaid.gov/policy/budget/cbj2007/lac/sareg.html. This list may be altered after publication of this book.

11. Thanks to journalist and investigator Anthony Fenton, this information was obtained directly from the National Endowment for Democracy. See n.6, p.160.

12. Narrative internal report about activities to the NED, authored by the Asociación Civil Liderazgo y Visión, 25 January 2005.

13. See Golinger, *The Chávez Code*, 80–84.

14. Carl Gershman and Michael Allen, "New Threats to Freedom," *Journal of Democracy* 17, no. 2 (April 2006): 36–51.

15. Ibid.

16. Ibid.

17. Ibid.

18. See http://www.wmd.org.

19. See the Freedom of Information Act, Exemption (b)(6).

20. See Golinger, *The Chávez Code*, 85–92.

4. Súmate in Bush's Hands

1. "Maria Corina Machado Holds a Media Availability Following a Meeting at the White House," May 31, 2005; available at http://www.whitehouse.gov.

2. Ibid.

3. View the document at http://www.venezuelafoia.info. Also see http://www.monthlyreview.org/bushvchavez.htm, Appendix 1, A1.4.

4. See http://www.ned.org/grants/venezuelaFacts.html.

5. Tom Casey, Acting Spokesman, U.S. Department of State, "Súmate Trial Decision," July 8, 2005, http://www.state.gov.

6. See http://www.monthlyreview.org/bushvchavez.htm, Appendix 1, A1.5.

7. See http://www.monthlyreview.org/bushvchavez.htm, Appendix 1, A1.6, A1.7, A1.8.

8. See http://www.monthlyreview.org/bushvchavez.htm, Appendix 1, A1.9, A1.10.

9. See Eva Golinger, *The Chávez Code: Cracking U.S. Intervention in Venezuela* (Northampton, Mass.: Olive Branch Press, 2006), 93–106.

10. See http://www.monthlyreview.org/bushvchavez.htm, Appendix 1, A1.11, A1.12, A1.13.

11. See http://www.monthlyreview.org/bushvchavez.htm, Appendix 1, A1.14, A1.15, A1.16.

12. See http://politica.eluniversal.com/2006/08/09/pol_art_09104A2.shtml.

13. See http://www.monthlyreview.org/bushvchavez.htm, Appendix 1, A1.17.

14. See http://www.monthlyreview.org/bushvchavez.htm, Appendix 1, A1.18.

5. Plan Balboa

1. See http://www.monthlyreview.org/bushvchavez.htm, Appendix 2 and Appendix 3, for documentary evidence of a U.S. military role in the coup against President Chávez and Plan Balboa.

2. See "Partnership of the Americas continues improving interoperability, relationships," *Navy Newstand,* May 5, 2006, https://www.navy.mil/search/display.asp?story_id=23603.

3. See "Zulia, another Washington Bid," *Granma International,* March 20, 2006, http://www.granma.cu/ingles/2006/marzo/lun20/13zulia.html.

4. Senator Richard Lugar commissioned the General Accounting Office to analyze and report on U.S. dependence to Venezuelan oil. The results indicated a high-level dependence that would be severely affected were a change in oil supply to occur. The GAO report stated the stoppage of Venezuelan oil supply to the U.S. would send the U.S. economy into a major crisis. See senate.gov/energy/venezuela/pdf/GAO_Report_Venezuela_Summary.pdf.

5. See http://www.monthlyreview.org/bushvchavez.htm, Appendix 2 and Appendix 3, for full details on U.S. military involvement in the coup.

6. William A. Arkin, "Pentagon to Venezuela: Who, Us?" *Washington Post,* November 3, 2005.

7. Carol J. Williams, "Dominicans Wary of U.S. Presence," *Los Angeles Times,* April 21, 2006.

8. Sergio Gómez Maseri, "Labores de espionaje de E.U. en América Latina han aumentado a niveles como las de la Guerra Fría," *El Tiempo,* April 25, 2006.

6. Curaçao: The Third Frontier of the United States

1. Ana Maria Salazar, Deputy Assistant Secretary of Defense for Drug Enforcement Policy and Support, testimony before the United States House Of Representatives Committee on Government Reform, Subcommittee On Criminal Justice, Drug Policy, and Human Resources, June 9, 2000, http://www.usinfo.state.gov/topical/global/drugs/canal.htm.

2. From a brochure distributed by U.S. military personnel to press and diplomatic visitors who toured the ship when it docked in Curaçao. See http://www.monthlyreview.org/bushvchavez.htm, Appendix 1, A1.19, A1.20.

3. See http://www.rense.com/general63/curaco.htm.

4. All this information is from the U.S. Navy website, http://www.navy.mil.

5. "USS *Stout:* A Formidable Presence to Defend the Interests of the United States," *La Prensa*, Curaçao, April 11, 2006. Original in Papiamento.

6. Ibid.

7. See fax sent by the U.S. Southern Command to Curaçao's Port Authority requesting the entrance of more than 100 warships during 2006 available at http://www.monthlyreview.org/bushvchavez.htm, Appendix 1, A1.21, A1.22, A1.23, A1.24.

8. "Amenazas contra Chávez: enseñar músculos y realizar provocaciones, maniobras militares en gran escala de la OTAN en el Caribe," por InSurGente/Prensa Latina, 7 Abril 2006, http://www.aporrea.org/dameverbo.php?docid=75833.

7. A Note on Asymmetric War and Wizard's Chess

1. See Qiao Liang and Wang Xiangsui, *Unrestricted Warfare* (Beijing: PLA Literature and Arts Publishing House, 1999), 109. See http://www.monthlyreview.org/bushvchavez.htm, Appendix 1, A1.25, A1.26, A1.27, A1.28, for maps of the region.

2. Ibid.

3. Max G. Manwaring, "The New Master of Wizard's Chess: The Real Hugo Chávez and Asymmetric Warfare," *Military Review*, September–October 2005, 46.

4. See article by Steven Matz and Douglas V. Johnson II, *Asymmetry and U.S. Military Strategy: Definition, Background and Strategic Concepts"* (Carlisle Barracks, Penn.: SSI, AWC, 2001), 5–6.

5. Manwaring, "The New Master of Wizard's Chess," 46.

6. Institute for Strategic Studies, "Venezuela's Hugo Chávez, Bolivarian Socialism, and Asymmetric Warfare," U.S. Army War College, October 2005, 20–21; http://www.strategicstudiesinstitute.army.mil.

7. Ibid., 23.

8. Ibid., 24–26.

9. Ibid., 26, citing Colonel Thomas X. Hammes, USMC, "4th Generation Warfare," *Armed Forces Journal,* November 2004, 40–44.

10. Institute for Strategic Studies, "Venezuela's Hugo Chávez," 6. "Chávez and Venezuela are developing the conceptual and physical capability to challenge the status quo in Latin America and to generate a 'Super Insurgency' intended to bring about a fundamental political and economic change in the region. Thus, as one sees Chávez's ideas developing and maturing, it is becoming more and more obvious that his bolivarianism is resonating with large numbers of people in Venezuela and the rest of Latin America—and that he should not be taken lightly."

11. Institute for Strategic Studies, "Venezuela's Hugo Chávez," 27.

12. Manwaring, "The New Master of Wizard's Chess," 47.

13. Ann Scott Tyson, "New Plans Foresee Fighting Terrorism Beyond War Zones: Pentagon to Rely on Special Operations," *Washington Post*, April 23, 2006.

8. Psyop War

1. Department of Defense, Doctrine for Joint Psychological Operations, Joint Publication 3-53, September 5, 2003.

2. In October 2003, the Pentagon published the "Information Operations Roadmap," which called for increased and improved psyops capabilities. "We must improve psyops. Military forces must be better prepared to use psyops in support of military operations and the themes and messages employed in a psyops campaign must be consistent with the broader national security objectives and national-level themes and messages. . . . In particular, psyops must be refocused on adversary decision-making, planning well in advance for aggressive behavior modification during times of conflict. Psyop products must be based on in-depth knowledge of the audience's decision-making processes and the factors influencing their decisions, produced rapidly at the highest quality standards, and powerfully disseminated directly to targeted audiences throughout the area of operations." Ibid., 6.

3. Ibid., I-1.

4. Ibid., ix–x.

5. See http://www.monthlyreview.org/bushvchavez.htm, Appendix 1, A1.29.

6. See http://www.monthlyreview.org/bushvchavez.htm, Appendix 1, A1.30.

7. Renae Merle, "Pentagon Funds Diplomacy Effort: Contracts Aim to Improve Foreign Opinion of United States," Washington Post, June 11, 2005.

8. See http:// www2.gwu.edu/~nsarchiv/NSAEBB/NSAEBB40/.

9. Wire story by the Associated Press, "Journalist Paid to Write for Military Web Site," February 4, 2005, published in various news media. See also "Media Advisory: Pentagon Propaganda Plan Is Undemocratic, Possibly Illegal," Fairness & Accuracy in Report, February 19, 2002.

10. Associated Press, "Journalist Paid to Write for Military Web Site," February 4, 2005.

11. Merle, "Pentagon Funds Diplomacy Effort."

12. Eva Golinger, The Chávez Code: Cracking US Intervention in Venezuela (Northampton, Mass.: Olive Branch Press, 2006), 102–104.

13. National Endowment for Democracy Grant No. 2005-373.0 to the Instituto Prensa y Sociedad de Venezuela, April 1, 2005–March 31, 2006 in amount of $74,950. See http://www.monthlyreview.org/bushvchavez.htm, Appendix 1, A1.31, A1.32, A1.33.

14. Venezolana de Televisión was broken into by opposition supporters on April 11, 2002, and taken off the air by force. It wasn't reopened until more than a day later, when Chávez supporters flooded the station in protest and eventually got it back on the air, just in time for Chávez's return to power. Catia TV, a local community media station, was also briefly shut down by then-Mayor of greater Caracas Alfredo Peña, a coup leader, in 2003.

15. Editorials, January 14, 2005, Washington Post and Wall Street Journal.

16. Department of State, Daily Press Briefing, January 14, 2005. Available at http:// www.state.gov.

17. Ibid.

18. Declarations made by Roger Noriega on the Voice of America radio station, February 4, 2005.

19. Questions & Answers, *Parade Magazine*, October 9, 2005.

20. Nancy Snow, *Information War: American Propaganda, Free Speech and Opinion Control Since 9-11* (New York: Seven Stories Press, 2003), 42.

21. See "Handling Chávez," Fox Fan, Fox News, http://www.foxnews.com, August 3, 2006.

9. Espionage and Sabotage

1. "Venezuela Expels U.S. Navy Attaché Over Spy Claims," Agence France Presse, February 2, 2006, http://www.defensenews.com/story.php?F=1509141&C=america.

2. Internal memo from the Anti-Drug Command of the Venezuelan National Guard, March 2005, provided to the author in confidence.

3. National Financial Intelligence Unit, *Internal Report of the Superintendent for Banks and Financial Institutions*, 2005. In author's files.

4. Ibid.

5. "Informantes denunciaron a la DEA ante el Ministerio Público," *El Nacional*, Caracas, 27 julio 2005.

6. 2005 Xinhua News Agency, Xinhua General News Service, November 29, 2005.

7. See http://www.rethinkvenezuela.com/downloads/burtonres.htm.

8. See http://www.aeinstein.org/organizations/org/2000-04rpt.pdf, p. 21.

9. See "About Bob Helvey" at http://www.aeinstein.org/organizations11db.html.

10. This testimony was taken in March 2006 in Caracas from an ex-Colombian paramilitary. I cannot confirm the veracity of all of his statements, though much of his testimony has proven accurate based on actions that have occurred over the past two years, Venezuelan law enforcement investigations, and press reports. I withhold the individual's name to protect his privacy.

10. Brownfield's Game

1. "Brownfield reconoce derecho de Venezuela a comprar armas pero con transparencia," *El Universal*, Caracas, 28 junio 2006.

2. "Departamento de Estado dice que incidence con embajador Brownfield es 'preocupante,'" EFE, 7 abril 2006.

3. See http://www.senate.gov/artandhistory/history/common/generic/VP_Richard_Nixon.htm and http://www.usatrivia.com/vpbinix.html.

4. See http://embajadausa.org.ve/wwwh018.html.

5. Internal memoranda from the U.S. embassy in Caracas to the State Department in Washington, D.C., authored by William Brownfield, 2005. Obtained through the Freedom of Information Act. Available in author's archives.

6. See http://64.233.161.104/search?q=cache:7zHylBhfwd8J:bakerinstitute.org/Pubs/testimony_peace.pdf+american+corners+department+of+state&hl=en&ct=clnk&cd=16.

7. See http://www.amcornersvenezuela.org/lecheria/lecheria.php.

8. See http://www.voltairenet.org/article130100.html.

9. See "Plan de Vuelo," por Nestor Suárez, http://www.cedice.org.ve.

Conclusion

1. "Professor Tinker Salas Visited by FBI Officials," March 24, 2006, http://www.tsl.pomona.edu/index.php?article=1447.

2. See http://www.citgo.com/CommunityInvolvement/HeatingOil.jsp.

3. *Declaration of Independence of the Thirteen Colonies of the United States of America*, July 4, 1776.

Index